# CONNECT CONVERT

*A comprehensive guide to attracting ideal customers, boosting sales, building client relationships, and maximizing referrals*

## MARGARITA EBERLINE

FOUNDER OF

# MARKETING BOSS

**13TH & JOAN**

For permission requests, write to the publisher, addressed "Attention: Permissions Coordinator," 205 N. Michigan Avenue, Suite #810, Chicago, IL 60601. 13th & Joan books may be purchased for educational, business or sales promotional use. For information, please email the Sales Department at sales@13thandjoan.com.

Printed in the U. S. A.

First Printing, June 2024

Library of Congress Cataloging-in-Publication Data has been applied for.

ISBN: 978-1-961863-25-5

# CONNECT CONVERT

*A comprehensive guide to attracting ideal customers, boosting sales, building client relationships, and maximizing referrals*

## MARGARITA EBERLINE

### FOUNDER OF

# MARKETING BOSS

# Contents

# Contents

# Dedication

To my five incredible children: Elijah, Emmanuel, Gabriel, Michael, and Joseph.

This book is dedicated to you, my precious boys. You have brought immeasurable joy, love, and laughter into my life. As your mother, I am forever grateful for the opportunities you have given me to test my negotiation and persuasion skills like never before.

From settling sibling disputes over toys to convincing you to do your chores, being your mother has been a constant exercise in finding creative ways to influence and guide. Through countless playful negotiations and heartfelt conversations, I have learned the art of connecting with others on a deeper level.

You have unknowingly served as my most outstanding teachers, shaping my ability to communicate effectively, understand different perspectives, and build meaningful relationships. Your presence in my life has transformed me into a more empathetic and skilled communicator.

As I share the secrets of legal sales within these pages, I want you to know that some of the greatest lessons learned and victories won were honed through my work experience with attorneys and the moments we shared together.

My love for you has fueled my drive to become the best version of myself as a mother and professional. Thank you for being my motivation and my constant source of inspiration. This book is a testament to the incredible journey we have embarked upon together. May it serve as a reminder that with determination, passion, and the power of persuasion, we can achieve anything we set our minds to.

# Foreword

*by Douglas Rohan, Founder/Owner of Rohan Law*

Over the years, I have witnessed firsthand in my firm and the firms run by colleagues I respect and admire the challenges that legal professionals face regarding marketing. It requires a unique skill set to navigate the complexities of the legal industry while effectively promoting one's services and connecting with potential clients. It is an honor to introduce this remarkable book on law firm sales, written by an extraordinary individual I have known for many years.

As an attorney and founder of Rohan Law, I have worked with numerous professionals dedicated to helping law firm owners grow their businesses. I have not seen or utilized anyone more talented than Margarita Eberline. She possesses a rare combination of skills that make her a proper Swiss Army knife in marketing and data analysis. And her ability to deeply connect with others and influence them is nothing short of astonishing.

Throughout the pages of this book, it is evident that she has poured her heart and soul into educating law firm owners and their teams. She understands the value of having a well-structured sales and intake system that can maximize the results of marketing efforts. Drawing from her vast experience and expertise, she provides practical insights and actionable strategies that can transform how law firms approach sales.

I have witnessed the author in action as she trained my team with many of these techniques long before she wrote this book. Her knowledge, expertise, and ability to captivate and motivate those around her impressed me. The impact of her training on my team and our overall business was significant. As she honed her training methods over the years, the benefits continued to grow, resulting in increased client intake and improved revenue streams. Since we first started using Margarita, we have seen 300% growth in our revenue.

Now, with the release of this book, I am excited to see the impact it will have on law firms across the country. Law firm owners, attorneys, and their teams will discover valuable information and guidance within these pages. From understanding the power of marketing to implementing a robust sales and intake system, this book offers a comprehensive roadmap to success. Good attorneys need to get exposure to as many potential clients as possible. There is plenty of business to go around, and I am happy to see clients in need hire honorable attorneys. Margarita can help you out-sell the law firm mills that focus on cash flow and profits over providing quality professional services to clients in need.

I am grateful to Margarita for her unwavering commitment to helping good law firm owners grow their businesses and serve more families. Her dedication and passion shine through every word, making this book an invaluable resource. I wholeheartedly endorse this book and encourage law firm owners to embrace its insights and strategies.

You and your team will be well-equipped to attract more clients and boost your profitability without sacrificing your values. Your journey to success starts here. Be sure to take advantage of the exercises throughout this book. With them, you can maximize your efforts and set yourself up for business success. Prepare to embark on a transformative journey to revolutionize your sales and marketing approach.

Here's to a prosperous future!

Best regards,
Douglas Rohan, Esq.
Founder/Owner, Rohan Law
Atlanta, Georgia

# Introduction

Welcome to *Connect, Convert: Response to Retainer Marketing and Sales Strategies for Law Firms.* Law firms are increasingly saturating marketing channels to attract customers in today's fast-paced and highly competitive landscape. But many law firms are doing so in vain by dumping thousands of dollars–even hundreds of thousands of dollars–to brand their firms and generate leads only to let them slip away. Getting the right customers to contact your law firm is the first step! To truly thrive, you and your team must connect, build trust, and convert leads quickly before those making the inquiry continue shopping with your competition.

*Connect, Convert* is your roadmap to success in this challenging environment. This ingenious guide unveils powerful strategies and techniques that empower lawyers and teams to attract ideal customers, increase case sign-ups, retain clients, and generate steady repeat business and referrals. The information is based on proven strategies designed to connect with and convert digital leads, which are some of the toughest to close.

With practical advice and real-world examples, this comprehensive resource equips readers with the tools to unlock their sales potential and achieve unprecedented success in the legal industry. Whether you're a seasoned attorney or a rising star, *Connect, Convert* will be your ultimate guide to becoming a force to be reckoned with in legal sales.

Law firms' support staff and receptionists can benefit significantly from the tips in this guide, as they are usually the first point of contact for most potential new customers. They will receive the tools to effectively engage potential clients and move them further in the sales process to a paid or free consultation, or a signed agreement.

In this transformative journey, discover simple yet effective techniques to leverage opportunities, qualify leads efficiently, and secure a client's  commitment. By implementing these strategies, you will position yourself and your firm to manage customers in a way that provides them with a positive experience, leading to better retention rates and a steady flow of referrals.

As a bonus, this guide covers ways to expand your customer base in the legal industry by leveraging marketing tactics and utilizing data-driven insights to attract ideal customers and follow up with them. You will learn to maximize your chances of success with messaging that predisposes potential new customers to say "yes" and by using marketing automation to follow up with and upsell contacts.

*Connect, Convert* will show you how to create a sales success cycle that transforms your firm's sales into a well-oiled machine. From connecting with potential clients to delivering exceptional service, each process step is carefully detailed, ensuring that you and your team have the knowledge and skills needed to excel. Let the book guide you as you navigate the challenges of the legal industry and build a thriving practice. Get ready to attract, convert, and retain customers like never before as you become a sales machine.

It's time to transform your legal sales approach and achieve remarkable success. Let's dive into *Connect, Convert* and embark on this exciting journey together.

Sincerely,
Margarita Eberline
Founder, Marketing Boss

# CHAPTER 1

# Sales Success Begins With Your Marketing

If you think the sales cycle begins when a potential new customer contacts your law firm, think again. The perception each potential new customer has of your law firm before they connect with you can set you up for success or failure. That perception is greatly determined by your firm's brand, including your word-of-mouth reputation, the look and feel of your marketing materials, and your advertising.

Set your firm up for success by carefully considering how you want your law firm's marketing materials to look and feel, what marketing channels you will use to advertise, and how you will manage your reputation online and in the community. Start by ensuring that your law firm has a brand guide that outlines guidelines for your logo, colors, and messaging for your ideal customer. For example, if you have a personal injury law firm, research your ideal customer's personality and preferences and ensure that your logo, colors, and messaging match, like a flower to a bee.

Next, think about what marketing channels to use. You might opt for online advertising on Google Ads, social media ads on Facebook and Instagram, or print materials like flyers and billboards. Ensure whichever channel you choose fits your brand and target audience and that the messaging will set proper expectations. For example, if you have a divorce law firm and want people to agree to a paid consultation, make sure your ads discuss the value your firm brings rather than the price. If your ads say "Competitive rates," the potential new customers that respond may not be as receptive to paying top dollar for an initial consultation.

You should also take steps to manage your firm's reputation. Ensure that what you advertise and intend to deliver matches what people say about you in the community and online. If you are advertising that you are experienced and one of the best but your Google reviews are full of one-star ratings, know that it will be harder to sell that way. If you have customer complaints about your service, ensure you address them as favorably as possible so there are no gaps between what you advertise and your reputation. It's harder to build trust when there are gaps between what you are selling and your brand.

Remember that your customer experiences and services are part of your marketing, so treat it as such. Many law firms sabotage their success by delivering sub-par service and trying to overcompensate with marketing. But more than marketing is needed to compensate for the negative customer experiences.

Ensure your customers consistently get a quality experience and service from you. Invest in customer support representatives who can handle complaints quickly and efficiently. Ensure they understand how to address these issues professionally. If you have poor customer service, if clients can't get a response from your firm quickly or professionally, they won't be likely to stick around for long. Any comments they make about you in conversations and online will negatively affect your brand and chances of attracting and signing up ideal customers.

You should have a documented marketing plan for your law firm that incorporates your brand guide and details the marketing channels you plan to use. Your plan should outline numerical goals like Key Performance Indicators (KPIs) and document how you will handle leads from each marketing channel. You should get help from a marketing expert to ensure that your marketing plan includes the best marketing tactics that will work for your firm. You can refer to the tips below to optimize your execution of marketing tactics in a way that sets you up for a smooth sales process.

# Optimize Your Website To Track And Convert Your Leads

Your law firm website should include a tracking phone number system that you can use to understand how visitors are interacting with your website. There are many platforms out there to choose from, like CallRail, that allow you to insert dynamic numbers that will give you data on how many times people visited your site before calling and will alert you and your team if someone is calling from your website. Knowing what website and page a potential new customer is coming from will give you valuable insight into what the potential new customer may be looking for or even just perceiving about your firm.

You should also include a live chat feature for potential new customers who are not ready to talk to anyone but may have questions. CallRail offers a chat feature, but there are others that you can integrate artificial intelligence into so potential new customers can get answers to common questions and even sign up without needing to talk to a member of your staff.

Website forms also provide a pathway for potential new customers to connect. You can use forms to let people message your team with questions or let you know they are ready to get started. You can even integrate online booking tools that allow people to book free or paid consultations online.

Integrating Customer Relationship Management (CRM) into your website can also help spruce up your forms. You can automate email responses each time a person fills out a contact form that alerts your team to a new lead. You can then add the contact to a sequence of emails sharing information about your firm via email, text, and even postcards and mailers.

Another great sales tool to add to your website, especially if you have an integrated CRM, is to offer at least one lead magnet. A lead magnet is a giveaway that provides value to your audience in return for their contact information. Some examples of lead magnets include free ebooks, opt-in courses, or discounts. You can use lead magnets to capture emails, nurture individuals making an inquiry further down the funnels and create additional sales opportunities with contacts who may otherwise pass through your website never to return. When a potential new customer is not ready to reach out but is interested in learning more, lead magnets offer them a way to access information without the pressure of taking that next step. At the same time, this gives your law firm a chance to nudge them toward being ready for the next step.

## Implement Digital Ads Best Practices To Prime Your Leads

If you plan to run digital ads on Google or social media, follow some of the same steps on a website. You should designate a unique tracking phone number so your team knows when a lead is calling from a digital ad and can treat them accordingly. You should also incorporate forms and chat options like on a website.

## Use Directories Like Google My Business To Widen Your Net

Google My Business and other directories are worth tracking with unique tracking phone numbers. Many directories also feature options to include different links so you can make special offers for the directories. Some directories like Google My Business and AVVO also feature options for potential new customers to send you messages through each platform. Ensure someone is responsible for checking the platforms daily, especially if they have a lot of traffic. You can also use tools to aggregate messages from multiple places to make monitoring more manageable for your team.

## Use Billboards To Brand Your Law Firm

Billboards are an excellent way for your law firm to gain exposure, but there are better ways to generate phone calls, especially if your advertised phone number is not easy to remember. Use a catchy vanity number whenever possible and track calls you may get directly from the billboards that way. But don't be surprised if you put up billboards and the phone calls from directories like Google increase because often potential new customers will make a mental note to call you, and then research you on the internet later and call from a digital marketing asset like Google My Business, your website, or social media.

## Best Practices To Incorporate Radio Into Your Media Mix

Like billboards, use a vanity number that is easy to remember to track calls and monitor other channels for leads on different media that indirectly respond to your radio ads. Many stations now integrate digital elements in their radio campaigns. If your radio deal includes that, use special links and other media tailored to the audience and campaign.

## Use Social Media Marketing To Connect

Similar to Google My Business and other directories, it's vital to monitor direct messages you may get from customers and potential new customers. You can use unique phone numbers in your content for each social media platform. You should also have a plan to monitor comments in your content and in any groups you are working with. Sometimes, people will ask for a call in a comment thread, or someone may refer to you or your firm in a group post or chat, so you may want to respond.

Setting up your marketing channels in a way that allows people to connect with you and your firm conveniently and seamlessly will position you for sales success. Offering multiple options and mediums for people to connect will increase your chances of converting leads. Making the process smooth will predispose them to say "yes" to whatever your firm is offering.

Many law firms miss out on maximizing their pipeline as much as possible because they don't offer more options. Others let leads slip by because they are not adequately monitoring all channels. Imagine writing to a law firm on AVVO and getting a response two weeks later. Would you want to sign up with that firm? Trying to sign up a client after they have had a clunky journey to your firm because they sent a message and no one responded for days will be a tough sell.

It is essential to take every possible step to follow these best practices to incorporate and monitor communication, whether it's email, website contact forms, chatbots, or messages on social media.

# Use Automation To Follow Up With Leads

When you incorporate a CRM or email marketing system with automation features, it gets a lot easier to follow up with leads later that don't convert right away. At a minimum, you should create a process at your firm to capture contact information. Suppose you capture information about the subject matter the potential new customer is inquiring about and track the outcome of a call. In that case, you can use this information to trigger automatic texts, emails, videos, postcards, etc., to get pushed out to the leads as a follow-up sequence. This can increase your case sign-ups while you sleep and save you time and money you might have otherwise spent on labor to follow up with them manually. The key is identifying the data points you need to track and building the messaging around that.

Automation is critical when it comes to lead nurturing. You can create automated emails and text messages or even postcards that get sent out based on specific criteria you set or data points you identify. For example, if a lead calls in inquiring about divorce services, you could have an automated email series created with content specifically related to that service go out for two weeks. This ensures that you constantly provide value and stay top of mind for potential leads. Additionally, with automated messages, you can A/B test campaign features to improve them constantly.

A/B testing is a valuable tool that can help you refine your marketing approach and customize your effort to nurture leads. You can experiment with different variables such as email subject lines, send times, content formats, images, videos, or call-to-action buttons. Test different options to gather data on what resonates best with your audience based on how they respond. This empirical approach allows you to make informed decisions backed by real user-engagement metrics. For instance, by A/B testing two different subject lines for the automated email series related to divorce services, you can identify which one generates a higher open rate and engagement, optimizing future communications for better performance. This methodical testing can help you improve your campaigns continually and help your leads feel how much you care about them and understand them.

Overall, automation is a potent tool you can use to connect with potential new customers when you create personalized and authentic experiences. You can also apply these same steps to follow up with leads that become clients to onboard them, too! In addition to helping you provide a better customer experience by proactively sharing information with customers, you will stay more visible with less effort. This can help you sign more repeat business and get more referrals from happy customers over time.

## Help Your Team Capture Every Lead With Standard Operating Procedures

When you allow multiple leads to connect with your law firm in a variety of ways, you create a broader customer base. Having efficient systems in place for capturing leads is akin to setting up a wide welcoming net. It ensures that no opportunity for new client engagement slips through. Law firms that want to scale should invest a reasonable amount of time and money in these systems, recognizing the potential for growth they bring. From intricate CRM tools to sophisticated social media monitoring platforms, these systems are designed to catch every inquiry and every interest shown in the firm's services. It's a digital-era marvel, enabling firms to reach out far beyond what traditional methods could have allowed.

However, here's the twist in the plot: While these systems are powerful, they're only as effective as the team using them. Many law firms face the challenge of keeping up with the multitude of channels through which leads can come. From direct emails and phone calls to social media messages and website inquiries, the array is vast. The reality is that without a clear, organized approach to monitor these channels, valuable leads can easily be missed. It's like having a state-of-the-art fishing net but not enough fishermen to check all corners. Some fish are bound to escape.

This is where the importance of a detailed blueprint document comes into play. Imagine a comprehensive map that not only identifies all potential lead sources but also outlines specific Standard Operating Procedures (SOPs) for handling these leads. Such a document should detail who is responsible for monitoring each channel; how to record a new lead, including the specifics of entering their contact information into your system; and the timeline for follow-up. This approach ensures that when a lead comes in through social media, for instance, there's no confusion about whether the person making the inquiry should be directly added to the CRM or first qualified through a preliminary exchange. The blueprint should clarify roles within the firm, identifying who is tasked with initial contact, who takes over for qualification, and how the lead is nurtured through the intake process.

Documenting these processes offers multiple benefits. It ensures consistency in how leads are treated, providing a uniform experience that reflects well on the firm. It also minimizes the risk of leads slipping through the cracks due to oversight or uncertainty. Most importantly, it allows the law firm to scale its operations efficiently. As the firm grows, having documented SOPs makes training new team members more straightforward, ensuring they can quickly become effective contributors to the firm's lead management efforts. In essence, this meticulous planning and documentation transform the potential chaos of lead management into a streamlined, efficient process that capitalizes on every opportunity for growth.

## Partner With Marketing Professionals

As you can probably gauge by now, creating a marketing strategy, setting up call tracking, selecting and implementing a CRM, and developing SOPs can be a lot of work. This chapter was designed to provide you with a brief overview so you have context as you dive into the sales strategies we put together for you. You should consider partnering with a professional marketing team or a chief marketing officer (CMO) company that can do the heavy lifting for you. Seek to collaborate with marketers who can enhance your firm's marketing efforts and develop a detailed marketing plan aligned with the firm's growth objectives and client acquisition goals.

A knowledgeable marketing team can identify the most suitable technology stack, including tracking software and form builders crucial for effective lead capture and management. They also play a key role in creating SOPs that clarify each team member's responsibilities in the lead management and nurturing process. When you partner with the right professionals, they can help you optimize your marketing machine and streamline operations so your law firm can attract more leads and convert them more easily. Even the best salespeople can struggle to convert poor-quality leads or leads that are missed because your systems are inefficient. By working with marketing experts, you and your team focus on connecting with and converting more leads with greater ease.

# CHAPTER 2

# Creating Standard Operating Procedures (SOPs)

This chapter expands on the Standard Operating Procedures discussed in Chapter 1. SOPs should be explicitly crafted to optimize sales and intake procedures within a law firm setting. In the dynamic and intricate landscape of legal services, the initial interactions with potential clients are pivotal moments that can shape the trajectory of a case and the overall client experience. From the first point of contact to the engagement of legal services, each step demands precision, professionalism, and a commitment to excellence.

This chapter presents a structured framework encompassing SOPs designed to enhance client acquisition, streamline intake processes, and foster lasting relationships built on trust and reliability. Whether you're a seasoned practitioner seeking to refine existing protocols or a newcomer eager to establish robust foundations, SOPs serve as invaluable tools for driving efficiency and delivering exceptional client service in law.

## Creating Your Own SOPs

Creating SOPs for sales at law firms can help streamline processes, ensure consistency, and enhance overall efficiency. Following are some tips to guide you through the process.

**Understand Your Sales Process:** Describe your current sales process from lead generation to closing deals. Identify each step involved, including client outreach, initial consultations, proposal submissions, negotiation, and closing.

**Document Each Step:** Write detailed descriptions of each step in your sales process. Include information such as the specific actions to be taken, the tools or software used, and any templates or documents needed at each stage.

**Define Roles and Responsibilities:** Clearly outline the roles and responsibilities of each team member involved in the sales process. This ensures everyone understands their duties and contributes effectively to the overall sales effort.

**Set Clear Objectives and Key Performance Indicators (KPIs):** Define measurable goals for your sales team and establish KPIs to track their performance. This could include the number of leads generated, conversion rates, average deal size, and revenue targets.

**Provide Training and Resources:** Develop training materials and resources to support your sales team in executing the SOPs effectively. This could include training sessions, instructional videos, process documents, and FAQs that address the customer journey and sales pipeline as well as the technology involved.

**Review and Refine Regularly:** Sales processes are not static and may need to be updated or refined over time. Schedule regular reviews of your SOPs to ensure they remain aligned with your business goals and reflect any changes in your sales strategy or market conditions.

**Ensure Compliance and Legal Considerations:** Since you're dealing with a law firm, ensure that your sales processes comply with legal or regulatory requirements. This includes adhering to ethical guidelines, client confidentiality, and data protection regulations.

By following these tips, you can develop effective SOPs for sales at your law firm that enhance productivity, ensure consistency, and ultimately drive business growth.

Still trying to figure out where to start? Examples have been added below to help you generate the best possible SOPs for your law firm sales.

## Initial Contact SOP

- Greet the potential client professionally and warmly.
- Gather basic information such as name, contact details, and reason for seeking legal assistance.
- Schedule an appointment for a consultation if necessary or ask for a signed agreement.
- Log all interactions in the CRM system.

## Consultation SOP

- Introduce the attorney and establish rapport with the client.
- Actively listen to the client's concerns and objectives.
- Provide relevant legal advice or guidance.
- Discuss potential strategies and outcomes.
- Clarify the next steps and any associated costs.

## Case Management SOP

- Create a case file for the new client in the firm's case management system.
- Assign tasks to relevant team members (attorneys, paralegals, etc.).
- Establish communication protocols and update frequencies with the client.

## Follow-up SOP

- Contact the client after the consultation to answer additional questions or address concerns.
- Send thank-you emails or letters expressing appreciation for choosing the firm.
- Schedule follow-up meetings or calls to keep the client informed about the progress of their case.

## Client Feedback SOP

- Regularly solicit feedback from clients about their experience with the firm's services.
- Use surveys or feedback forms to gather constructive criticism and testimonials.
- Analyze feedback to identify areas for improvement and implement necessary changes.

## Documentation and Compliance SOP

- Ensure all client interactions and communications are accurately documented in the firm's records.
- Adhere to legal and ethical guidelines regarding client confidentiality and data protection.
- Regularly review and update SOPs to comply with changes in regulations or best practices.

These SOPs can serve as a starting point for you to develop your own. You should add additional details that outline the tasks and subtasks involved with screenshots, diagrams, and any visual aids that can help your team complete the tasks consistently. The aim with these SOPs is to streamline your law firm's sales and intake processes, ensuring consistency, efficiency, and excellent client service.

# CHAPTER 3

# Knowing Your Core Skills  Assessing Your Sales And Intake Abilities

To carve a clear path to where you need to be, you must know where you are now. In law firm sales, understanding your strengths and areas for growth is crucial for success. This chapter will guide you through a self-assessment exercise, helping you gain insight into where you stand in the three core skills essential for excelling in law firm sales. You can develop a roadmap for further growth and achieve remarkable results by appreciating your strengths and identifying areas that require improvement.

## Assessing Your Skills

Before you begin, please note that no one is perfect. There is always room for growth and development. Even if you perceive yourself as the best in any area, understanding the areas where you excel and those that need improvement is vital for continuous progress.

### I Am An Excellent Sales Person.

Excellent people in law firm sales possess a unique blend of communication skills, legal knowledge, relationship-building expertise, negotiation prowess, and a results-driven mindset. They continuously strive for excellence, adapt to change, and leverage their deep understanding of the legal industry to forge strong client connections, secure new business, and drive revenue growth for their firm. With their exceptional abilities and unwavering dedication, they play a vital role in the success of their law firm and contribute to its continued growth and prominence in the market.

## I Am Good At Signing People Up.

Whether you are guiding people to a consultation or to sign an agreement, you possess the skills to persuade people to take the next step. It requires the art of persuasion, building trust, clear communication, active listening, persistence, and professionalism to get a client's commitment. It means that you can foster meaningful connections, address client needs, and successfully guide potential clients through engaging the law firm's services in whatever role or capacity you occupy. Ultimately, this expertise is pivotal in enabling individuals to take the next step toward finding the legal solutions they seek.

**CONNECT & CONVERT ACTIVITY**

### Rate Yourself

*Complete this activity with the free worksheet from the Marketing Boss App Connect Convert Resource Library.*

Read the definitions below of the top three skills high-performing law firm sales professionals possess. Once you have read each description, ask yourself how true each statement is about you. Then rate yourself on a scale of 1-10 based on how accurate the statements are about you, with one being completely inaccurate and 10 being very accurate:

## I Am The Best In My Field.

How confident are you in your professional expertise? If you are a receptionist, do you consider yourself one of the best? If you are a lawyer, how confident are you in your skills and accomplishments? No matter your role at the law firm, being the best in your field encompasses various aspects, including confidence in your professional expertise and a commitment to continuous improvement. Whether you are a receptionist or a lawyer, striving to be the best means consistently delivering exceptional results, honing your skills, and staying ahead of industry trends. This mindset drives excellence and fosters a passion for continuous learning and growth, ultimately setting you apart as a top performer in your chosen profession.

Once you complete this exercise, note how you have rated yourself. As you continue reading through the book, pay attention to tips and exercises that can help you improve your strength in each area where you gave yourself less than a 10 rating. Recognizing that not reaching a perfect score is a common experience can be liberating. It's important to understand that many people do not achieve a perfect score and, in fact, may never do so. This reality isn't a reflection of failure but an opportunity for growth. The goal isn't to attain perfection but to identify where you currently stand so you can enhance your personal best.

By honestly assessing where you stand in each skill area, you will gain valuable insights into your current abilities and uncover the areas that require further development. This process allows you to focus on these areas throughout this book. Feeling bad about not achieving the highest marks only detracts from the learning process. Instead, view each less-than-perfect rating as a stepping stone toward improvement. Remember, improvement is a personal journey. What matters most is your commitment to growing and enhancing your skills over time.

In fact, it's worth appreciating how much self-awareness and self-acceptance form the bedrock of personal development. Acknowledging your current skill levels without harsh self-judgment is a powerful act of self-compassion. By understanding and accepting yourself as you are, you create a solid foundation for growth. This acceptance doesn't mean you're settling for less from yourself, rather it means you're starting from a place of honesty and kindness toward yourself. Once you've established this connection with yourself, you're better positioned to connect with others.

People are naturally drawn to authenticity and the unmistakable confidence that radiates from individuals who possess a deep understanding and acceptance of themselves. This profound self-connection does more than just bolster self-esteem. It fundamentally transforms the way you interact with the world around you. It sharpens your communication skills, enabling you to articulate your thoughts and ideas more clearly and persuasively, making every word resonate with genuine conviction. Furthermore, this self-awareness fosters a heightened capacity for empathy, allowing you to perceive and respond to the emotions and needs of others with remarkable sensitivity and understanding.

In the context of connecting with and converting potential new customers, these qualities become invaluable. They empower you to create messages that truly speak to your audience's desires and challenges, building trust and rapport that can seamlessly translate into successful conversions. Beyond the professional realm, this deep personal authenticity and confidence enrich your personal life by laying the groundwork for more meaningful and fulfilling relationships. Whether in casual encounters or lifelong connections, the ability to engage sincerely and empathetically makes you a magnet for positive interactions and bonds. Cultivating a deep connection with yourself not only elevates your professional success but also significantly enhances the quality of your social and personal life, creating a harmonious balance that benefits all areas of your existence.

# CHAPTER 4

# Creating Exceptional Service Experiences For Potential New Customers

Taking the time to think about and prioritize customer service is essential. What comes to mind when considering good customer service and its significance when interacting with potential new customers in law firm sales? Let's explore how exceptional service can differentiate your firm and establish long-lasting relationships with potential new customers and clients. While there are some general best practices you can use, the best way to help potential customers feel well cared for is when you serve them based on your unique personality and natural strengths.

## The Importance Of Service In Law Firm Sales

In the competitive landscape of law firm sales, providing outstanding service is crucial in securing new clients. Service goes beyond delivering legal expertise. It involves creating exceptional experiences that instill confidence, trust, and a sense of being well cared for. It creates emotional responses where potential new customers feel valued, understood, and supported. These feelings make them more likely to choose your firm over competitors.

# Defining Service In The Context Of Potential Customer Interactions

Regarding potential customer interactions, service involves understanding and addressing your client's needs, concerns, and expectations throughout their journey with your firm. It requires active listening, empathy, and effective communication to build rapport and establish a foundation of trust. By providing personalized attention and demonstrating a genuine commitment to their success, you create a service experience that sets your firm apart.

# Exercise: Developing Your Personalized Plan For Exceptional Service

To create exceptional service experiences that align with your personality and come naturally to you, we will walk you through an exercise that helps you identify your unique strengths and develop a plan of action.

### Step 1: Self-Assessment

Reflect on your personality traits, skills, and strengths that lend themselves to providing exceptional service. Consider your ability to empathize, communicate effectively, and problem-solve. Consider past experiences where you felt you provided excellent service and analyze what made those interactions successful.

### Step 2: Understanding Customer Needs

Gain a deep understanding of your potential customers' needs, expectations, and pain points. Conduct research, interact with clients, and seek feedback to identify common themes and areas where you can provide added value. Are there patterns in what they are saying or asking or in their tone that you can anticipate and address? This knowledge will guide your service approach and help you tailor your interactions to meet customer expectations.

### Step 3: Creating Your Action Plan

Based on your self-assessment and understanding of customer needs, create an action plan that outlines specific steps to enhance

## Crafting Your Service Blueprint

*Complete this activity with the free worksheet from the Marketing Boss App Connect Convert Resource Library.*

In the spirit of enhancing our approach to serving clients, I invite you to deepen your understanding of customer service by aligning your personal values with your firm's mission. Take a moment to journal about how you personally prefer to serve customers. Take a moment to ponder the unique aspects that define your approach to service. What aspects of what the firm represents are you most passionate about? How can you uniquely ensure each client feels valued and understood? By documenting these reflections, set a clear and personal intention toward service for any potential new customers at your law firm. This process is not just about self-discovery. It's about crafting a service blueprint that resonates with who you are and what you stand for. Engage deeply with this activity and together, let's redefine excellence in service, one personal insight at a time.

the service experience for potential customers. Consider leveraging your strengths to address their concerns, offer personalized solutions, and make them feel genuinely cared for. You may make it a habit of sharing personal experiences that potential new customers can relate to. For example, if you work at a personal injury firm where you get calls about auto accidents and have also been in a crash, you can add that personal experience to your action plan. You can make it a habit to mention to potential new customers who call about a Personal Injury (PI) case that you understand what it's like because you were also in a crash. Other actions include active listening or additional resources to help them feel like you are ready and willing to support their legal journey.

## Step 4: Implementation And Evaluation

Put your action plan into practice and observe its effectiveness. Continuously monitor and evaluate the impact of your service initiatives through client feedback, customer satisfaction surveys, or other measurable indicators. Adjust your approach to continually improve and refine how well you serve each person you interact with.

Prioritizing service in law firm sales and its role in creating exceptional experiences for potential customers will help you establish, maintain, and grow long-term relationships. With an effective plan in place, your law firm will be able to demonstrate its commitment to excellent service every time a client or potential customer interacts with your team—from the initial contact through the resolution of their legal problem. Law firms must recognize that client service should be a top priority. Understanding the importance of service, conducting a self-assessment, identifying customer needs, and developing a personalized action plan can enhance the service experience and build strong relationships with potential clients. Remember, exceptional service is not just about what you do but how you make your potential customers feel valued, supported, and well taken care of.

# CHAPTER 5

# The Three Critical Actions For Law Firm Sales Calls  Reassure, Connect, And Document

Your law firm may have a checklist of items that must happen on each sales call or interaction. Regarding sales during the initial call or consultation, you should accomplish three critical actions during every law firm sales call: Reassure, Connect, and Document. While it is essential to have flexibility in managing dialogue for each potential new customer, these actions ensure consistency in the customer experience and lay the foundation for successful case sign-ups. We will explore achieving these goals without relying on a scripted conversation, allowing you to engage with potential new customers and authentically build meaningful connections.

## The Power Of Reassurance in Law Firm Sales Calls

Reassurance builds trust and confidence during sales calls. Potential clients may be seeking legal assistance during challenging times, and it is crucial to reassure them that your firm has the expertise, resources, and dedication to address their needs. By actively listening, empathizing, and addressing their concerns, you can alleviate their worries and instill a sense of trust. You can make statements such as, "We have helped others like you," or "Yes, we handle those types of cases here," to reassure the potential new customer that they are in good hands with your firm.

## Connecting On A Personal Level

Establishing a personal connection is key to fostering a positive rapport with potential clients. While avoiding a rigid script, engaging in genuine conversations that allow you to understand their unique circumstances and build a connection based on empathy and understanding is essential. By demonstrating sincere interest, asking thoughtful questions, and actively listening, you can create a connection beyond the surface level and solidify their confidence in your firm. You can make "I" statements such as, "I am going to do everything I can to help you," or "I am glad that you called."

## The Importance Of Documenting Call Details

Effective documentation is critical to law firm sales calls. Not only does it ensure accuracy and clarity, but it also enables seamless collaboration with colleagues and provides a comprehensive record of client interactions. By diligently documenting relevant details such as the individual's concerns, case specifics, and next steps, you can facilitate efficient follow-up, track progress, and provide consistent service throughout the client's journey. Even if the lead is not qualified, taking down their contact information will enable you to stay in touch with them through marketing lists, newsletters, etc., and stay top-of-mind when they are ready to purchase legal services.

## Strategies For Accomplishing The Three Critical Actions

While maintaining flexibility in your approach, there are several strategies you can employ to consistently accomplish the three critical actions during law firm sales calls.

1. **Reassure**
   - Actively listen to the potential new customers' concerns and validate their emotions.
   - Provide clear and empathetic explanations of how your firm can help address their legal needs.

## Unveiling Your Innate Strengths

*Complete this activity with the free worksheet from the Marketing Boss App Connect Convert Resource Library.*

This thought-provoking exercise is designed to help you become more aware of where you stand when it comes to the three most critical actions that you need to perform during every interaction with a potential new customer. Take a moment to journal about which of the three critical actions comes more naturally to you and why. This introspective activity is not just about recognizing your strengths. It's about gaining clarity on what is effortless for you, thereby pinpointing areas ripe for development. By understanding where your innate abilities lie, you create a roadmap for enhancing those skills that require a bit more polish. This exercise serves as a vital step in your journey toward becoming a more effective, attuned, and empathetic service provider. Draft your thoughts, reflect deeply, and discover the power of awareness in transforming the way you connect and convert potential new customers into signed cases for your law firm.

- Share success stories or case examples demonstrating your firm's expertise and track record.
- Offer reassurance about the process, timelines, and potential outcomes, addressing any specific concerns they may have.

2. **Connect**
   - Engage in genuine conversations by asking open-ended questions and showing a sincere interest in their situation.
   - Empathize with their experience and acknowledge their legal issue's impact on their lives.
   - Personalize your approach by tailoring your responses to their unique circumstances and concerns.
   - Use active-listening techniques to understand their perspective and demonstrate that you value their input.

3. **Document**
   - Take thorough and accurate notes during the call, capturing essential details and action items.

- Utilize a CRM system or other documentation tools to maintain consistency and organization.
- Summarize the main points discussed during the call and confirm understanding before engaging.
- Share relevant information with colleagues or team members for seamless collaboration and follow-up.

By consistently achieving these goals without relying on a set script, you can create a customer experience that is reassuring, personal, and well documented. Building trust, establishing connections, and maintaining accurate records lay the groundwork for successful case sign-ups and long-term client relationships. Remember, while each call will be different, focusing on these three actions can provide a consistent and exceptional experience for potential clients, setting your law firm up for success.

# CHAPTER 6

# Creating Customer Avatars To Enhance Connection And Conversion

Creating customer avatars or personas can help you visualize and mentally and emotionally prepare for connecting with potential new customers. You may have these already created as part of your marketing plan and strategy but if you do not, you can use these tips to create one or more avatars. If you have avatars in your marketing plan but notice potential new customers that don't fit the avatars, you can also use these tips to add to the list of avatars. By understanding the types of customers you can expect to interact with and their pain points, you will be better equipped to anticipate their needs, empathize with their emotions, and effectively reassure, connect, and convert them. We will explore the steps in creating customer avatars and how they can enhance your sales approach.

## The Power Of Customer Avatars In Law Firm Sales

Customer avatars or personas are fictional representations of your ideal customers. They capture key customer segments' key characteristics, pain points, motivations, and behaviors. By creating these avatars, you gain a deeper understanding of your target audience and can tailor your approach to address their needs and concerns. Customer avatars are potent tools to visualize and mentally prepare for connecting with potential new customers.

## Step 1: Identifying Customer Segments

Identify the different customer segments you may encounter in your law firm's sales process. Consider demographics, legal needs, industry, and other relevant criteria differentiating each segment. This segmentation allows you to create more targeted and personalized avatars.

## Step 2: Gathering Customer Insights

To develop accurate and realistic customer avatars, gather insights about your target audience. You can conduct market research, analyze client data, or simply converse with existing clients. Explore their pain points, motivations, challenges, and expectations when seeking legal assistance. These insights will help you empathize and connect with potential customers.

## Step 3: Crafting Customer Avatars

Based on the customer segments and insights gathered, craft individual customer avatars. Give each avatar a name, assign demographic characteristics, and delve into their personal and professional backgrounds. Dive deep into their pain points, goals, fears, and desires. Consider their emotional state and mindset when seeking legal support. The more detailed and accurate your avatars are, the better prepared you will be to connect with potential new customers. You can use this list of characteristics and write them down. You can make a list of these characteristics or write a paragraph summary.

**EXAMPLE 1:**

Karen is between 35 and 45 and is looking for a divorce lawyer in Ventura County, California. She is a nurse and makes decent money, so she can afford to pay the retainer, but her primary concern is being able to communicate at odd hours because of her schedule. She is the primary breadwinner and will likely need guidance to ensure she doesn't overpay in alimony.

## Empathy in Anticipation— Profiling the Client

*Complete this activity with the free worksheet from the Marketing Boss App Connect Convert Resource Library.*

Construct a detailed profile of your ideal client, focusing on preemptively understanding their thoughts and feelings. Meditate on your prospective clients' mindset and plan to tailor your communication and explanation of legal services to resonate on a personal level, fostering empathy and trust before the initial conversation begins. This effort will help you ensure that every client feels understood and valued from the moment they decide to reach out to your law firm. If your law firm manages multiple practice areas, consider repeating this exercise for each area, identifying at least one customer type per practice area. This approach allows for a more nuanced understanding of potential clients across diverse legal needs, ensuring that your firm's communication strategy is effectively tailored to each specific audience.

**EXAMPLE 2:**

Lamont is between 25 and 55 and is a Black male in Colorado. He was arrested, has a record, and is afraid of having to do jail time again. He is also concerned about discrimination by the police and the court system. He is looking for a criminal defense attorney he can trust not to judge him and to look out for his rights.

## Step 4: Utilizing Customer Avatars In Sales Calls

Integrate customer avatars into your sales process. Before each call, review the avatar relevant to the potential customer segment you will interact with. Visualize the avatar, put yourself in the potential client's shoes. Consider how they may feel and what they need from your law firm. Use this mental and emotional preparation to guide your conversations, anticipate their concerns, and tailor your responses to effectively reassure and connect with them.

## Step 5: Evolving And Refining Customer Avatars

Customer avatars should evolve dynamically over time. Gather feedback, learn from client interactions, and update your avatars accordingly. As you gain more experience and insights, refine the avatars to reflect your target audience's changing needs and expectations. This ongoing process ensures your connection and conversion strategies remain relevant and practical.

Customer avatars can help enhance connection and conversion in law firm sales. You can establish more robust connections and increase conversion rates by creating avatars representing your target audience, visualizing their pain points, and mentally and emotionally preparing to engage with potential customers. Remember to continuously refine and update your avatars based on real-time insights and feedback. By incorporating customer avatars into your sales approach, you will be well-prepared to anticipate customer needs and provide tailored reassurance and connection, ultimately driving success for your law firm.

# CHAPTER 7

# Master The Art Of Phone Greetings For Law Firms

The initial greeting in a phone conversation sets the tone for the entire interaction, especially for a law firm where trust, professionalism, and compassion are paramount. Within the first few seconds of the call, the caller's psychological state is heavily influenced. The initial moments of the conversation consequently serve as a critical foundation for building rapport and trust. A warm, professional, and reassuring greeting can immediately put the caller at ease, making them feel valued and respected. This positive first impression is crucial in a legal context, where clients are often dealing with stressful or sensitive issues. It establishes a sense of confidence in the law firm's capabilities and also fosters a conducive environment for open communication.

## Greetings Best Practices Extend Beyond Phone Calls

The psychological impact of this initial interaction cannot be overstated. It lays the groundwork for a trusting relationship, which is essential in any legal proceeding. The way that you greet potential clients can significantly impact the tone and outcome of your conversations, whether they happen on the phone or online. By incorporating best practices and developing personalized greeting scripts for each communication channel, you can create a positive first impression, establish rapport, and set yourself up for success.

The best practices below are outlined for phone greeting because that is the most common medium that potential new customers use to contact law firms. But keep in mind that the tenets of a strong greeting extend beyond phone conversations. The best practices can and should be adapted for written communications as well—be it through social media messages, emails, or web chats. In today's digital age, first interactions are increasingly occurring online, making it imperative to extend the same level of professionalism, warmth, and assurance in written form.

Just as with phone greetings, the initial message to a lead or potential new client also sets the stage for the interaction. A thoughtfully crafted written greeting can convey empathy, professionalism, and attention to detail, fostering a sense of trust and respect right from the outset. This approach not only mirrors the positive psychological effects of a good phone greeting but also caters to the preferences of clients who may favor digital communication. By applying these greeting strategies across all platforms, law firms can ensure a uniformly excellent first impression, irrespective of the medium through which a potential client reaches out.

## Best Practices For Greeting Potential New Customers

To ensure effective and personalized greetings, consider the following practices.

### Research Cultural Norms

For starters, you should take into account the potential new customer's language and cultural background. You should aim to demonstrate respect and value for their individuality. It's critical to be aware of the cultural norms and etiquette associated with various languages and regions. These insights will enable you to tailor your greetings and appropriately avoid unintentional cultural missteps.

## Use Appropriate Language

Keep in mind that in law firm sales calls, potential new customers are often nervous. Creating a comfortable and reassuring environment from the start is crucial. So greeting them in a language they don't understand can introduce anxiety into the conversation right off the bat. On the flipside, if you can greet potential new customers in their native language, this can instantly establish a connection and make them feel more at ease.

What if you work at a multilingual firm and you do not know what the caller's preferred language is prior to answering the call? You have several options. One is to implement specialized phone lines designated for specific languages based on your advertising campaigns. For instance, if your firm is conducting Google Ads in Spanish, establishing a unique tracking phone number exclusively for these ads can be incredibly effective. This setup makes it safe to assume that calls received through this particular number are predominantly from Spanish-speaking individuals. With this method, your firm can pre-emptively identify the caller's language preference, enabling a more personalized and seamless communication experience right from the first greeting.

Using tracking numbers like this can streamline the process for the law firm staff and allow them to prepare and engage in the most appropriate language immediately. This is assuming that the law firm staff speaks their language of course. If they do not speak the language, a warm friendly English greeting is appropriate.

If you are handling a call with someone who does not speak English, keep in mind that this can be intimidating for them and make an extra effort to ensure that your tone conveys sincerity and professionalism.

What if you do not know the language and/or do not have any way of knowing the caller's language before you pick up the phone? You can opt for a bilingual greeting such as, "Thank you for calling Acme Law. How can we help you? ¿Cómo le puedo ayudar?" This approach shows your willingness to accommodate their language preferences and helps foster a positive and welcoming atmosphere. It can be effective whether or not you can continue the call in the caller's language. If you can speak Spanish or whatever the second language is, your bilingual greeting will serve as an invitation for the caller to continue in their native tongue. If you do not speak the language you can gently redirect them to English, letting them know that you are acknowledging their language and culture with an effort to greet them as best as you can.

## Personalize Your Greeting

Whenever possible, address potential new customers by their name. This shows attentiveness and indicates that you value their individuality. If you recognize their name by potential new customer ID, you can go with that or politely ask them with a statement such as, "My name is [insert your name]. What's yours?" Using a person's name in conversation is a powerful psychological tool deeply rooted in our cognitive and social wiring. It's more than just a label for identification. A name carries with it a sense of individuality, identity, and personal recognition.

As you leverage this technique, be mindful of cultural naming conventions and preferences. When in doubt, ask permission to call them by their first name, last name, or nickname. For example, if the caller ID says Dave Johnson, you can say something such as, "Hi Dave. May I call you Dave or should I call you Mr Johnson?" In many cultures around the world, addressing someone by their last name rather than their first is a sign of respect and formality.

This practice varies significantly across different countries, regions, and contexts and is often influenced by social hierarchies, traditions, and the level of formality in relationships. Following are a few examples where people might prefer to be called by their last names.

### EAST ASIAN CULTURES (E.G., JAPAN, KOREA, CHINA)

In these countries, it's customary to use the family name followed by a honorific suffix (like "-san" in Japanese, "-nim" in Korean, or a respectful title in Chinese) when addressing someone, especially in formal settings or when the relationship is not intimate. The use of last names signifies respect and maintains social harmony.

### GERMANY

Germans are known for their formality, especially in business and professional settings. It is common to address people using their last names preceded by a title (e.g., Herr for Mr., Frau for Mrs./

Ms.) until a closer relationship is established or one is invited to use the first name.

## RUSSIA

In Russia, using the first name and patronymic (a name derived from the father's first name) is common in formal situations. However, addressing someone by their surname can also be a sign of respect, especially in professional or official contexts.

## HUNGARY

Hungarian names are traditionally given in the order of last name followed by first name. In formal settings, it's usual to address someone by their last name, reflecting respect and politeness.

## FRANCE

While more informal interactions may allow for first names, addressing someone in formal or business settings by their last name—especially with a preceding title (Monsieur for Mr., Madame for Mrs., or Mademoiselle for Ms.)--is seen as a sign of respect.

**CONNECT & CONVERT ACTIVITY**

### Crafting Your Signature Greeting

*Complete this activity with the free worksheet from the Marketing Boss App Connect Convert Resource Library.*

Now that you are familiar with these best practices for a greeting, you are ready to create a personalized greeting script that can help you maintain consistency while allowing room for individuality. The following is a step-by-step approach.

## Express Genuine Interest

Show genuine interest in the potential new customer's well-being and reason for contacting the law firm. Ask how you can assist them and actively listen to their response. This demonstrates empathy and establishes a foundation for a productive conversation.

## Be Clear And Polite

Speak clearly and enunciate your words to ensure potential new customers understand you. Use polite language and courteous phrases, such as

"Please" and "Thank you" to convey professionalism and respect. Feel free to politely ask potential new customers to repeat or clarify anything that is not clear so they know you are paying attention and are interested in what they have to say.

## Identify Your Objectives

Determine the key objectives you want to achieve with your greeting. These may include making a positive first impression, establishing rapport, and setting the tone for a productive conversation.

## Consider Language Preferences

Determine if you can greet potential new customers in multiple languages. If so, identify the languages most commonly spoken by your target audience and incorporate appropriate greetings in those languages into your script.

## Tailor For Individuality

Customize your greeting script to reflect the target audience's unique needs and characteristics. Consider combining any specific legal expertise or services that set your firm apart.

## Practice And Refine

Take the time to practice your greeting script to ensure it flows naturally and sounds authentic. Seek feedback from colleagues or mentors and make necessary refinements to enhance its effectiveness.

## Can't Think Of Anything?

If you struggle to come up with something, you may be overthinking things. Following are a few examples of greetings you can try out that may help you identify what can work best for you through trial and error. Remember to speak naturally and avoid sounding robotic.

### If Your Law Firm Is Bilingual

"Thank you for calling ACME Law. How can I help you? *¿Cómo le puedo ayudar?*"

## If Your Law Firm Is Not Bilingual

"Thank you for calling ACME Law. How may we serve you today?"

Whether you draft your greetings to try out or use these examples, get excited about applying and refining your personalized greeting script on calls. Now that you know these best practices, you will notice a difference in the tone set at the beginning of each call. You can set a positive tone and establish rapport with potential new customers by incorporating cultural awareness, using appropriate language, personalizing your greetings, expressing genuine interest, and maintaining clarity and politeness. Developing a well-crafted greeting script enhances consistency while allowing space for individuality, setting you up for success in connecting with potential clients and driving law firm sales. Remember, a warm and professional greeting is the first step in building a solid foundation for a successful client relationship.

# CHAPTER 8

# Screening For Potential New Clients

## Avoiding Costly Mistakes During The Screening Process

Properly distinguishing between existing leads and potential new clients in the law firm sales process can be trickier than you think. Many law firms miss out on valuable opportunities due to sloppy screening practices. We will review common mistakes made during the screening process that can hinder your chances of converting leads into clients. Navigating conversations effectively and asking the right questions allows you to gather the necessary information to screen and qualify leads without accidentally discarding promising prospects. Let's delve into the art of effective lead screening.

## The Significance Of Proper Lead Screening

Proper screening of leads is crucial for maximizing your law firm's conversion rates. It allows you to identify and prioritize potential new clients while ensuring existing leads receive the appropriate attention and follow-up. By avoiding common mistakes in the screening process, you can avoid losing out on valuable opportunities and develop a more efficient and effective sales approach.

To avoid missing out on potential new clients, it is essential to be aware of and address common mistakes made during the screening process. Following are some of these mistakes.

**Failing To Gather Sufficient Information:** Neglecting to ask pertinent questions and gather essential details about the potential new customer's legal needs and background can result in incomplete lead assessments and missed opportunities. Ensure that your team is well versed in the practice areas you handle, what information you need to qualify a case, and what factors make for an ideal case. For example, if you handle family law cases in a specific county, your team must be trained to ask what county the potential new client is in.

**Not Clarifying The Purpose Of The Call:** When faced with digital inquiries from individuals who may have mistakenly contacted your law firm while seeking another, it is important to handle the situation delicately. If a potential new customer says, "I would like to talk to ACME law," and your firm is NOT ACME law, resist the temptation to say, "No, sorry, wrong number." Instead of immediately dismissing them, ask questions such as, "Is this about a new or existing case?" This approach allows you to uncover potential opportunities and assist potential new customers effectively. If the potential new customer says they are calling about a new case, proceed to qualify them.

**Misjudging The Value Of Existing Leads**: Existing leads from individuals who have contacted the firm before should not be overlooked or assumed to have already received the information they need from your law firm. Each interaction is an opportunity to nurture existing relationships and potentially generate new business. Approach existing leads with the same level of attentiveness and care as you would with potential new customers. Take the time to ask questions and listen rather than assuming you already know what they need. This can help put your firm one step ahead of competitors regarding client retention.

It takes practice and understanding an ideal case for your law firm to be effective. You should complement your experience and expertise with general strategies to help you distinguish between existing leads and potential new clients by doing the following.

**Actively Listening:** Pay close attention to the potential new customer's words, tone, and underlying needs. By actively listening, you can gather valuable information and ensure that you fully understand their situation.

**Asking Probing Questions:** Seek clarification by asking targeted questions about the potential new customer's legal needs, timelines, and expectations. These inquiries allow you to assess the potential value of the lead and tailor your approach accordingly.

**Diversify Your Approach:** Every potential new customer is different. While it's nice to have a canned list of questions you can ask verbatim, you should diversify the way you ask the same questions between potential new customers. You can ask the same question the same way to two potential new customers. One may understand your question the way you mean it, and the other may not. So pay attention to that and be prepared to ask questions differently as needed. For example, if you are a personal injury firm trying to determine if an accident was the potential new customer's fault and you ask, "Were you at fault?" and the potential new customer says, "No," you may want to ask the same question a different way just to be sure. You can ask, "Did you get a citation?" The potential new customer may say "Yes," suggesting they may have been at fault.

**Provide Clear Information:** Clearly communicate your law firm's services, expertise, and the benefits of working with you. This clarity ensures potential new customers understand what you can offer and helps them self-identify as fit for your firm. If you are a divorce attorney and explain that you only work cases in Acme County, the potential new customer can tell you, "Yes, I live in that county" or "No, I do not live in that county."

When you apply these best practices to screen potential new clients properly during their first or second call, you can effectively identify and assess each potential new customer's ability to work with your law firm. Additionally, it may help you prevent misunderstandings and ensure that the customer experience you provide is smooth and pleasant.

# CHAPTER 9

# The Power Of Empathy In Client Communication

Many law firms miss out on qualifying and signing up new clients simply because attendants are distracted, multitasking, stressed, or simply not present mentally and emotionally during a call with a potential new customer. Making it a priority to show empathy and provide a good customer experience can help. By showing genuine understanding and care for the potential new customer's needs, you can build trust in that person quickly and easily.

Empathy can also help you easily stand out in the competitive world of law firms since a top complaint about law firms is a lack of emotion and connection. Empathy can help build trust, establish long-lasting relationships, and be a game-changer for your firm's success.

Making a genuine connection with potential new customers is easier than you think once you learn to be fully present and empathetic, even during distraction and stress.

## Understanding The Potential New Customer's Perspective

Take some time to imagine that you are a potential client reaching out to a law firm for the first time. You may feel anxious, overwhelmed, and uncertain about what lies ahead. It's crucial to remember that the person on the other end of the line seeks support during a difficult time. By putting yourself in their shoes and considering their emotions, you can create an immediate bond and demonstrate your commitment to helping them navigate their legal challenges.

## Be Present In Every Interaction

In our fast-paced world, it's easy to get caught up in distractions and feel overwhelmed by the job's demands. However, mindfulness and being fully present are essential when engaging with potential new customers. If you are feeling distracted or on back-to-back calls, you can do a simple breathing technique that takes seconds to snap you into focus. Close your eyes and take a deep breath. As you do, clear your mind and intend to focus solely on the conversation at hand. By giving your undivided attention, you allow yourself to effortlessly connect emotionally with potential new customers as you show respect and validate their concerns, making them feel heard and understood.

## Be Authentic As You Engage In The Conversation

Imagine for a moment that the potential new customer is a relative, a friend, or someone you care about, and adjust your energy accordingly. Empathy begins with listening to the potential new customer's story, concerns, and needs. Switching gears from a professional energy to a more personal one can help you do this. Avoid interrupting or rushing through the conversation. Instead, take a genuine interest in their situation. Show empathy through verbal cues such as paraphrasing and phrases such as, "I understand" or, "I can hear how this is difficult for you." You can even make it a habit of saying, "I hear you," knowing that by acknowledging their emotions and validating their experiences in whichever way comes more naturally to you, you build trust and establish a solid foundation to move the conversation forward through the sales process.

# Responding With Compassion

Once you have absorbed the potential new customer's story, respond with genuine compassion. If you are fully present in the conversation, this comes naturally. Offer reassurance, highlighting that they are not alone in their struggles. Share relevant success stories or examples that showcase how your firm has helped clients facing similar challenges. Demonstrating your track record and expertise instills confidence. Recognize the signs of stress and burnout and implement self-care strategies to maintain a healthy mindset. In addition to breathing and awareness exercises, try stretching, walking, drinking water, eating when you are hungry, and if necessary, talking to someone you trust about how you are feeling. These activities will enable you to approach each interaction with renewed energy and genuine empathy, ensuring every client and potential new client receives the best support.

Empathy is a powerful tool to set your law firm apart from the competition. You create a connection beyond legal expertise by putting yourself in the potential new customer's shoes, being fully present, and responding with genuine compassion. Remember that each potential client seeks understanding and support during a challenging time. By mastering the art of empathy, you can establish trust, build long-term relationships, and ultimately sign up more cases. Empathy can be a valuable tool that drives the success of your law firm.

If you are struggling with empathy, you are not alone. Many professionals in the legal field struggle with genuinely empathetic interactions, particularly due to the inherently analytical and logical nature of their work. Lawyers are trained to think critically, focus on facts, and often maintain emotional detachment to argue their cases effectively. This mindset, while invaluable in court and case preparation, can inadvertently carry over into client interactions, creating a barrier to empathy.

The high-stress environment of law practice, compounded with a heavy workload, can leave little room for lawyers and anyone working at a law firm to step back and engage empathetically. The pressure to meet deadlines, manage client expectations, and achieve favorable outcomes can overshadow the need to connect on a human level.

## Building Your Empathy Toolbox

*Complete this activity with the free worksheet from the Marketing Boss App Connect Convert Resource Library.*

Take a moment to think about statements that come naturally to you that express empathy. Consider phrases that resonate with understanding, care, and genuine concern. Use language that conveys warmth, offers solace, and acknowledges the emotions of your callers. By creating this personalized empathy toolbox, you equip yourself with verbal tools that can transform interactions, making every potential new customer feel valued and understood. You will be better equipped to create habits that strengthen the bonds you forge with potential new customers.

Overcoming these barriers requires a conscious effort to cultivate empathy as a skill. There are some effective connection strategies further ahead in this book that can also help you with empathy. Overall, practicing regular reflection and mindfulness can also help you become more attuned to your own emotional responses and the feelings of others, enhancing your ability to connect with clients on a personal level.

Ultimately, developing empathy is about appreciating that people want and need to work with law firms that are willing to address their emotional needs alongside their legal ones.

# CHAPTER 10

# Establishing Value  The Key To Successful Client Progression

It's common for people to verbally agree to move forward in the next step of a law firm's sales cycle and not mean it. Potential new clients will say yes to a free consultation and then not show up. They will agree to a paid consultation and then not sign up. They will agree to sign an agreement and then not follow through. They will sign an agreement and not pay. All of these types of behaviors are a symptom of a lack of perceived value. Taking extra steps in the conversation to build value will help minimize this phenomenon of a client not progressing.

In addition to building trust and showing empathy as outlined in the previous chapters, demonstrating value before asking customers to take the next step in the sales process will make them more likely to follow through without second-guessing their decision. Whether it's a consultation, a contract signature, or any other commitment, resisting the temptation to rush forward is crucial. Instead, take extra steps to show value, gain trust, and ensure clients are ready to move forward and commit.

## Reassure Clients That They Called The Right Place

When engaging with potential clients, it's essential to make them feel confident that they have chosen the right law firm. Highlight your firm's attributes, such as years of experience, successful outcomes, and specialized expertise. This reassurance will instill trust and set the stage for a yes they will follow through with. If you are new and can't think of any attributes to cite, something as simple as letting the caller know that you care, can be enough to reassure them that they called the right place. You can say something such as, "David, I am so glad that you called so we can help you. I am going to do everything I can for you."

## Talk Up Your Team To Build Confidence In The Next Step

As you progress through the sales process, it's crucial to introduce the people on your team whom potential clients may interact with next. Highlight their qualifications, experiences, and dedication to providing exceptional service. By showcasing your team's expertise, you build confidence and reinforce the value of moving forward with your firm. For example, if you are scheduling an appointment for a potential new customer with an attorney, take a few extra seconds to say something about the attorney such as, "John is easy to talk to. You will love him," or "John has a lot of experience with cases just like yours." Take a moment to list your team members and jot down some things you can say to compliment them. Remember who your target customers are and what might impress them most.

## Share Relevant Success Stories Demonstrating Relatability

One powerful way to establish value is by sharing success stories or case studies similar to the potential client's situation. Describe how your firm helped others overcome similar challenges, highlighting positive outcomes and the impact of services on their lives. With these strategies, you can effectively overcome objections and increase your closing rate, ultimately driving success for your law firm.te and alleviating their concerns.

## Remember to Practice Self-Care

It is much easier to be present at the moment and show empathy consistently when practicing self-care. You can support others more efficiently when your needs are taken care of. Be aware of how you are feeling and if you are anxious, stressed, or feeling any negative emotion, take a moment to acknowledge your emotions and process them before you interact with a potential new customer and inadvertently bring negative energy into the conversation. For example, if the phone rings and you are in the middle of a stressful task, take a pause to breathe and shift your focus to the caller before you pick up the phone. Taking a few seconds to do this can make a difference.

## Demonstrating Personal Care And Commitment

Another way to establish value is by expressing genuine care for the potential client's well-being. Let them know you are personally committed to helping them find the best possible solutions. This doesn't mean you have to promise them legal help that you are not qualified to give. It's more of a personal commitment to do your best in your role at the firm. Address their concerns and offer empathetic support throughout the conversation. You can solidify the foundation of trust and value by showcasing your personal dedication to their success.

## Time The Next Steps Conversation

While demonstrating value is essential, gauging the client's readiness to move forward is equally important. Pay attention to their verbal and non-verbal cues, such as enthusiasm, engagement, and questions. Sometimes, the cue is a sense of relief, so look for that. When you perceive that they are genuinely committed and ready to progress, confidently offer the next steps in the sales process. This approach ensures a smoother transition and increases the likelihood of successful client progression.

## Some Potential New Customers Intend To Agree And Not Follow Through

Sometimes potential new customers will prompt you to move forward with the sales process, but beware of signs that this can backfire. If you have not established value and the potential new customer is asking for pricing information, they are not likely to move on to the next step and/or follow through if they do say yes to you. Letting the customer lead you to talk about price prematurely can cost you. Instead, acknowledge their question and address value. For example, you can say, "Before we get into pricing, I think it's important for you to know that we have an excellent success rate with cases like the one you describe." Keep building value until you sense the emotional cues of excitement or relief. Those emotions usually mean they are truly ready.

If they are not excited or relieved and are done talking, you can also try asking them questions to get them to talk about objections or issues they may not be articulating yet. For example, you can ask, "What other questions can I answer for you?" to get them to reveal more of what is going on in their mind and identify thoughts and objections that can creep up later and lead them to ghost you and the firm.

For example, suppose you've presented your legal services to a potential new client and their response seems lukewarm or non-committal. You might probe deeper by saying, "From our discussion, is there any aspect of our services that you're unsure about or would like more information on?" This question encourages them to articulate specific doubts or misunderstandings they may have about your services.

Imagine you're discussing representation in a personal injury case and after explaining your firm's approach, the client becomes quiet. By inviting them to share their thoughts with a question like the one above, they might reveal, "I'm just worried about the costs involved and how long the process might take." This opens up an avenue for you to address these specific concerns directly, perhaps by explaining payment structures or providing a general timeline based on similar cases.

Sending the potential new customer an agreement when they still had this fear rattling in their mind may have led them to ignore the paperwork and not sign it, even though they may have stated they were ready to move forward. Instead of letting this happen, you can probe deeper and provoke conversations about hidden objections and misunderstandings with questions. In doing so you can demonstrate your attentiveness and commitment to transparency, while significantly reducing the likelihood of them ghosting due to unresolved concerns or misconceptions.

Once you have built enough value and they are either relieved or excited to work with you and your firm, you can introduce them to the next steps. Their emotional state of excitement and relief are signs that they are more likely to follow through if they agree to an appointment, sign a contract, or take whatever other action you want them to take in the sales process.

## Assume They Want To Move Forward

If you have qualified the lead, built up the value of the law firm, and reassured them you care, then they are likely ready to hear your instructions for what's next. You don't need to ask if they want to move forward. You can simply assume it and guide them through the steps. Rather than asking questions such as, "Would you like an appointment?" or "The consultation is X dollars, is that ok?" simply assume it and say things such as, "I have appointment A available or B. Which would you prefer?" or "The consultation is X dollars. Would you prefer to pay with a credit or debit card?"

## Ask Them To Write Things Down

Asking clients to write things down helps build value by creating a sense of formality. Also, writing things down can encourage the client to be more committed to doing what they need to do next to move the sale forward. Asking your potential new customers to take a moment to write things like an appointment date and time, a list of things you need them to do, or whatever other instruction is related to a step you need to take can help create value and help the sale stick. Plus, it allows them to refer back and track what they must do before the meeting or appointment.

Encouraging clients to write down appointment times or action steps during a conversation can sometimes lead to moments of silence, which might feel awkward at first. This pause occurs as the client shifts their focus from listening and speaking to the physical act of looking for a pen and paper or writing. While such silence may initially seem uncomfortable, it's important to become comfortable with this quiet space. Embrace the awkward silence as an opportunity for both you and the client to process the conversation so far. The moment for reflection is well worth it as an effective means to secure the client.

## Help Them Picture Themselves Working With You

Visualization is a powerful tool that taps into the subconscious mind and can greatly influence our actions and outcomes. When people visualize themselves doing something before actually doing it, they are more likely to value the experience and follow through. By describing simple scenarios, such as driving to your office or what to expect during a consultation, you help potential clients see themselves in those situations. This prompts them to build excitement and envision themselves taking the necessary steps, making them more likely to take action. Visualization creates a sense of familiarity and comfort, boosting confidence and motivation. By leveraging the power of visualization, you can inspire potential clients to overcome any hesitations and proactively engage with your law firm.

Visualization is a psychological tool. Understanding that there are psychological factors that influence purchasing decisions will help you as you perfect your client acquisition skills. Strategies that focus on both the monetary value and emotional benefits are ideal. Remember that clients who seek legal assistance also need to feel safe. Aim to provide assurance that the services they're paying for meet their unique needs and provide real value for their investment as you build trust. When clients perceive that a law firm's services are tailored to offer substantial benefits that address their specific situations, and they hear it from someone they like and trust, they are more likely to say "Yes" and mean it.

You can motivate potential new customers to choose you and your law firm with confidence by establishing value with these strategies before asking potential clients to take the next step. You will notice that as you do this, there will be an increase in the number of clients who follow through with the agreed-upon things. Know that by reassuring them they have chosen the right place, highlighting your team's expertise, sharing relevant success stories, and expressing genuine care and value, you are well on your way to becoming a sales machine for your law firm. Remember to assess the client's readiness and offer the next steps only when they show genuine interest and commitment. Following these principles will increase the chances of successful client progression and build long-lasting relationships based on trust and mutual value.

# CHAPTER 11

# Overcoming Common Objections

If you follow the recommendations in this book, you should not have very many objections to overcome. If you do get an objection from a potential new client who is a likely qualified lead, it is going to fall into one or more of the following categories: Price, needing to think about it, needing more time, or needing to consult someone else.

## Addressing Price Concerns

Price objections can arise when potential clients perceive the cost of your services as too high or if they have budget constraints. The key phrase here is "perceived value." To convince them of your value, emphasize the expertise, experience, and successful outcomes your firm has achieved. Present the long-term benefits and potential cost savings your services can offer. You can also discuss value in terms of potential problems your law firm can help them avoid. For example, if you sell criminal legal services, you can explain the risks of showing up to court without legal representation. Even when clients may have real budget constraints, they can get creative and find ways to fundraise because the perceived value of avoiding extreme risks motivates people.

You can also refer your potential new customers to funding companies or share stories about creative ways that people can get the money they need for legal services. For instance, some law firm clients may fundraise among friends and family to get their family members out of jail.

As you respond to pricing objections with points about value and share creative funding solutions, it is important to stay professional and empathetic. You want to show empathy if the client shares sincere and heartfelt insights about their limited budget. You should acknowledge the client's budget constraints but don't apologize for your pricing or lower your rates. Instead, explain clearly why your service is worth the cost and how it can help them in the long run. Showing that you understand their needs and the financial reality they face is essential in showing that your law firm is a professional, trustworthy source of legal services.

You can also offer payment options if that solution is within your business model, such as installment plans or prepay discounts. But it should be the last thing you try. There are benefits and drawbacks to consider when you play with pricing in a negotiation. While discounts and payment plans give clients more flexibility in making the service accessible, it can send a subtle message that your services are worth less than you originally quoted.

Most of the time, pricing objections are easy to overcome when you properly build up the perceived value of your legal services. So before you reduce your fee, explain why the service is worth its cost and how the client will benefit from hiring a law firm. Law firms are often seen as a reliable source of legal expertise and can be valuable to any business. Showcasing this can go a long way in getting the deal closed.

## Handling The Need To Consult Someone Else

When potential clients mention the need to consult with someone else before making a decision, it's crucial to acknowledge and respect their process. Provide them with the necessary information and resources to share with their trusted advisors. Offer to schedule follow-up meetings or calls to address any additional questions or concerns they may have after consulting with others. By showing understanding and support, you build trust and increase the likelihood of reaching a favorable outcome.

If you sense that they are not sincere but rather offering an excuse , then you can also try nudging them a bit with questions. Assuming the person they want to consult is a spouse, you could ask, "What sort of questions do you think your wife/husband might ask?" or, "What do you think your spouse's concerns might be?" These questions will prompt the potential new client to expand on or reveal objections they might not have articulated yet. By doing this, you will better understand their hesitancy and be able to address it directly.

Remember to remain empathetic and encouraging throughout the conversation and strive for mutual understanding. If necessary, take a step back and allow them space or time to think before resuming the conversation. Demonstrate patience, as they might be worried about making a decision they could regret. You want to be there to guide their thought process and not pressure them or manipulate them.

By following these tips, you can effectively address any objections and questions your potential new client may have. You can also gain insights into the mindset or concerns of your prospects. Being attentive and understanding of their needs will help you to make a lasting impression and eventually close the deal. It's also a nice way to ensure they got all of their questions and concerns out of the way and are happy with the information you provided.

Once you get to the point where you have answered the questions and concerns that their co-decision maker may ask, you can ask them to move forward and see if their answer changes. You can say something such as, "What do you think your husband/wife might think about moving forward now that all of the concerns he/she may have been addressed?" If they indicate the answers are acceptable, then you can ask them to proceed knowing that their spouse or other person would be in agreement.

## Overcoming The "Think About It" Objection

When potential clients express the desire to think about it, it's important to address their concerns and provide further clarity proactively. Ask open-ended questions to understand their hesitation and engage in active listening. Then highlight your firm's specific benefits and solutions that directly address their needs and concerns. Share success stories or case studies demonstrating how your firm has helped clients in similar situations. You create a sense of urgency and empower them to make informed decisions by showcasing the value and outcomes they can expect.

If you are unsure what they want to think about, it's also ok to simply ask, "What is it that you would like to think about exactly?" or, "If you take some time to think about things, what do you think might happen?" All these questions are about getting more information you can address more clearly. People usually use these objections when they are stuck trying to make a decision or have other objections or questions that they are not open about for whatever reason.

People who are too shy to say "No" and explain why might be the most challenging to handle. If you start by understanding why they are hesitant in the first place, it will help you assess them and what kind of information or actions to take next. It could be as simple as providing more examples of cases where your law firm proved the best choice for a case like theirs.

## Allowing Ample Time For Consideration

Some potential clients may request more time to consider their options right after saying they need to give their decision more thought. You can try some of the same questions above for this objection. Ask, "How much time" or, "Why do you need more time?" Note that in either case, this can be an opportunity to strengthen the relationship and build value.

Is there any value in acting now versus taking more time to think? If so, make sure you express those points. Again, it's not about pressuring people into a decision they are not ready to make. It's about helping them flush out their thoughts. Sometimes you may be doing them a disservice if you agree to give them more time before trying to help them see the value in acting now. For example, if they call you because they were charged with a crime and they have court in a few weeks, taking more time to think can hurt them. Your law firm will have less time to negotiate with the prosecutor before the court date.

Express empathy while offering ongoing support during their decision-making process. Give them insights on the risks of waiting and the benefits of taking action now. It can help to have additional resources handy to share such as articles, educational materials, or testimonials to help them gain further confidence in choosing your law firm. This is where having automated messages set up can

## Build an Objection Navigation Chart

*Complete this activity with the free worksheet from the Marketing Boss App Connect Convert Resource Library.*

When people object, it's important to consider the underlying reasons for their objection. Is it fear, a lack of trust, or an inability to see the value you're offering? Once you understand the root of the objection, you should tackle it accordingly. Make a list of the objections you encounter most frequently in the left column, and in the right column, write how you plan to overcome them. This activity is designed to sharpen your problem-solving skills and enhance your ability to address concerns with confidence and efficiency. By systematically breaking down objections and pairing them with tailored responses, you're setting yourself up for smoother interactions. Keep an open mind and empower yourself to turn every objection into a stepping stone towards building stronger, more meaningful customer relationships.

help with the sales process without wasting too much time. Offer to have someone on the team call them back if they'd like more information or need assistance in deciding further. Reassure them that you and your team are here to help and provide a solution for their situation. Make sure to keep this conversation as honest and transparent as possible so they can make an informed decision.

Overcoming objections is not just a skill but an art in the sales process for law firms, embodying both practice and confidence at its core. Plan to navigate roadblocks that may otherwise cost your law firm a new signed case by addressing common concerns with confidence. As you tackle price concerns and counteract the "think about it" objection, consider that you will get better at diffusing their hesitation as you practice. Remember that in doing so, you're guiding your potential new customers to choose the best law firm—yours. Embrace the process as a means to build trust and create profound relationships with people who want to feel like they are in good hands.

## CHAPTER 12

# Reprogram Beliefs That Don't Serve You

Almost every single receptionist, paralegal, lawyer, or other person who talks to potential new clients in a sales intake capacity has at least one limiting belief that is affecting their ability to realize their full potential to sign up more cases. You can improve your ability to sign up more cases by applying strategies only to the degree your greatest limiting belief allows.

## The Power Of Limiting Beliefs

Limiting beliefs can act as significant roadblocks, hindering our chances of signing up clients and achieving our full potential. Take a moment to think about and make a list of any limiting beliefs that you have about yourself and your abilities. Then think about the impact of these beliefs and take steps to counteract them with positive, empowering thoughts. By addressing and transforming these limiting beliefs, you can unlock your full sales potential and drive success in your law firm.

Limiting beliefs are, simply put, beliefs that limit your potential. Some common ones at law firms are, "I am not a good salesperson" or, "I don't know enough to help people." These beliefs may feel and appear to be very accurate, but they are not. If you address them, they can ensure your confidence and support your ability to sign up cases. These beliefs create a negative mindset that affects your interactions with potential clients, eroding trust, and hindering your persuasive skills. It's essential to recognize the power of these beliefs over your success and take steps to counteract them effectively.

## Identifying And Challenging Limiting Beliefs

The first step in overcoming limiting beliefs is to identify and challenge them. Pay attention to your thoughts and self-talk when engaging in sales activities. Notice any negative beliefs that emerge and assess their validity. Question the evidence supporting these beliefs and challenge their accuracy. Often, these beliefs stem from past experiences or misconceptions and do not reflect your true capabilities.

Once you have identified your limiting beliefs, replacing them with positive affirmations that align with your true capabilities is essential. For example, if you believe you are not a good salesperson, replace that thought with one that feels true and better but that serves you such as, "I genuinely care about people, and that helps me build the trust necessary to guide them through the sign-up process." If you struggle with the belief that you don't know enough, counteract it with the affirmation that you are the best at your job and that your expertise is enough to help people.

These examples help you think about your beliefs and how you can counteract them. Transforming limiting beliefs requires awareness and new beliefs you can internalize to take their place. You can affirm daily, repeating positive statements that negate your limiting beliefs. Surround yourself with supportive colleagues or mentors who can provide encouragement and help you challenge and reshape your beliefs. Over time, through repetition and consistent effort, your positive affirmations will replace the limiting beliefs, allowing you to approach sales confidently and authentically.

Limiting beliefs can be significant roadblocks to success in sales for law firms. You can unlock your full sales potential by recognizing their power, challenging their validity, and replacing them with positive affirmations. Embrace the belief that you have what it takes to be a successful salesperson, leveraging your care for people and expertise in your field. With consistent practice and reinforcement, you will cultivate a positive mindset that empowers you to build trust, sign up cases, and thrive in your role. Remember that addressing and transforming your limiting beliefs will pave the way for personal growth, enhanced sales performance, and long-term success in your law firm.

In fact, continuously working on your mindset and beliefs is an essential aspect of personal and professional development that will serve you well in the high-pressure environment of law. The legal profession challenges individuals not just intellectually but also emotionally and psychologically. It is therefore crucial for you to engage in practices that foster mental resilience, adaptability, and wellness. Therapy or coaching can play a pivotal role in this process, offering tailored strategies to cope with stress, manage work-life balance, and enhance emotional intelligence.

Therapy provides a confidential space for lawyers and legal staff to explore personal and professional challenges without judgment. It can be instrumental in identifying and addressing sources of stress and anxiety that are prevalent in the legal field. Therapy helps in developing healthier coping mechanisms, improving relationships both within and outside the workplace, and ultimately leading to a more fulfilling career. On the other hand,

**CONNECT & CONVERT ACTIVITY**

### Belief Transformation Map

*Complete this activity with the free worksheet from the Marketing Boss App Connect Convert Resource Library.*

Make a list of the negative thoughts and limiting beliefs that hinder your confidence and performance, especially those that emerge during calls with potential new customers. On the opposite side, write positive affirmations and empowering beliefs that directly counteract each limiting thought. By consciously recognizing and reformulating these barriers into sources of strength, you will enhance your personal growth and significantly improve your interactions with clients. This activity is a powerful step toward altering your mindset, enabling you to become a more positive, confident individual who builds trust and connects with others with ease.

coaching focuses on professional growth and development, helping individuals to set and achieve career goals, improve leadership skills, and enhance decision-making abilities. It complements therapy by focusing on the application of strategies to achieve professional success while maintaining mental and emotional health.

Engaging in therapy or coaching signifies a commitment to self-improvement and acknowledges the importance of mental health in achieving professional excellence. It is a proactive approach to addressing the inevitable stresses of legal work and can significantly contribute to a more balanced and satisfying career. Furthermore, investing in mental health through therapy or coaching can lead to broader cultural change within the legal profession, promoting an environment that values and supports the well-being of its members.

Start identifying and working through some mindset limitations that may be holding you back, and definitely consider continuously working on your mindset. The value of repeating the exercise below often and seeking therapy or coaching cannot be overstated for legal professionals. It enhances personal well-being and enriches professional performance. If you work in a law firm, you can benefit from prioritizing mental health as a critical component of professional development.

CHAPTER 13

# Set Goals And Crush Them

Mastering your numbers can make it fun to pursue sales success at your law firm. Knowing critical metrics such as the number of calls you can handle, qualified leads identified, sign-ups for the next step, and conversion rates to paying customers empowers you to make data-driven decisions and optimize your sales strategies. Consider the importance of knowing your numbers, tracking them effectively, and letting them guide you to improving the steps you take to achieve sales success.

## Quantifying Your Performance

### Know Your Capacity

To maximize your sales efforts, it's crucial to understand your capacity in terms of the number of calls you can handle. Analyze your workload and time management skills to determine a realistic number of calls you can comfortably manage daily, weekly, and monthly. By setting a clear capacity goal, you ensure you are not overwhelmed and can give your full attention to each call, maximizing your chances of converting leads into paying customers.

### Track Qualified Leads

Identifying qualified leads is a crucial step in sales. By tracking the number of qualified leads you identify, you gain insights into the effectiveness of your prospecting efforts. Monitor various lead sources, such as referrals, marketing campaigns, and networking events to identify which channels generate the most qualified leads. This data lets you focus your resources and energy on the most fruitful avenues, improving your overall lead-generation strategy.

## Monitor Sign-Ups And Conversion Rates

Tracking the number of sign-ups for the next step, whether a consultation or further engagement, provides valuable insight into the effectiveness of your sales pitch and nurturing process. Analyze the conversion rates from sign-ups to paying customers to identify areas where potential clients may fall through the cracks. Understand the reasons behind any drop-offs and implement strategies to improve conversion rates, such as enhancing your follow-up process or addressing common objections more effectively.

## Apply Strategies And Celebrate Improvements

Once you have a clear understanding of your numbers, you can enjoy the process of applying the sales strategies you have learned. Use your data to experiment with different approaches, fine-tuning your techniques based on the insights gained. As you see improvements in your numbers, celebrate your successes, no matter how small. Recognize that incremental progress is key to long-term growth and maintain motivation by focusing on the positive impact of your efforts on your sales performance.

Knowing your numbers is critical for achieving sales success in law firms. You gain valuable insights into your sales performance by quantifying your capacity, tracking qualified leads, and monitoring sign-ups and conversion rates. With this information, you can make data-driven decisions, optimize your strategies, and continually improve your results. Embrace applying what you have learned, and celebrate the small wins. Remember that by mastering your numbers, you empower yourself to achieve consistent sales success and drive growth in your law firm.

## Score Your Calls Based On Key Best Practices

Score your calls and evaluate your effectiveness at implementing the best practices. You can use a scorecard system to audit the call recordings of client interactions and quantify how well they go. By rating key factors on a scale of 1-10, such as greeting effectiveness, qualification skills, empathy, name usage, reassurance, contact information gathering, appointment scheduling, value establishment, team positivity, and assumptive selling, you can identify areas for improvement and maximize your sales effectiveness.

## Establish A Scorecard System

Establishing a scorecard system encompassing critical factors in successful sales conversations is vital to auditing your phone calls effectively. Use a rating scale of 1-10 for each factor consistently. This scorecard system provides a structured approach to analyzing your performance and allows for objective assessments.

**Greeting—Evaluate Greeting Effectiveness:** Consider how effectively your greeting sets a positive tone. Assess your ability to make a friendly first impression, which helps build rapport and establishes trust from the onset of the call. Consider the greeting script's tone of voice, enthusiasm, and professionalism when assigning a rating.

**Qualifying—Assess Qualification Skills:** Effective qualification is crucial in determining the potential value of each case. Rate how well you ask probing questions to understand the potential new customer's situation and legal needs. The better you qualify the cases, the more efficiently you can allocate your resources and focus on the most promising opportunities.

**Empathizing—Evaluate Empathy And Reassurance:** Empathy plays a vital role in connecting with potential new customers on an emotional level. Rate how well you demonstrate empathy by actively listening, validating their concerns, and showing genuine understanding. Additionally, assess your ability to reassure potential new customers by addressing their fears or uncertainties and confidently providing them with your services.

Build trust by reassuring that you care and are personally glad they called.

**Preparation—Prepare the PNC to say yes:** Evaluate your ability to effectively establish the value of your services, highlighting the benefits and outcomes clients can expect when working with your firm. How well do you do this before you schedule appointments or asking them to sign an agreement?

**Assurance—Create an Atmosphere of Assurance and Trust:** By assuming the sale, confidently stating the reasonable price, and expressing the assumption the potential clients are eager to avail themselves of the valuable legal services, you can create an atmosphere of assurance and trust. This approach encourages potential clients to recognize the value being offered and increases the likelihood of them saying "yes" to the legal services.

**Personalization—Analyze Name Usage And Contact Information Gathering:** Personalization is key to building rapport and trust. Rate how frequently you use the potential new customer's name during the conversation to show attentiveness and create a personalized experience. Set an expectation that you will follow up and assess your ability to gather accurate contact information, ensuring you have the means to follow up effectively.

**Reassurance—Appointment Scheduling And Establishing Value:** Assess how effectively you establish the value of your services, highlighting the benefits and outcomes clients can expect when working with your firm. This approach encourages potential clients to recognize the value offered and increases the likelihood of them saying "Yes" to the legal services. Assume the sale, assume the price is reasonable, and assume they want to pay.

**Commitment—Assess the Team and Secure the Sale:** Evaluate your ability to promote a positive image of your team and convey confidence in its expertise. Rate how well you highlight the strengths and capabilities of your colleagues. Additionally, assess your use of assumptive selling techniques, such as assuming the sale and confidently guiding the potential new customer toward the next step.

# Customize The Scorecard List To Your Law Firm

If your law firm has unique processes for quality interaction, add them to your list of things that make up your scorecard. For example, if you have a divorce law firm and it's essential for your team to gather information about what county the potential new customer lives in, add that to your scorecard.

Another example of a custom rating you can track for your scorecard is if you have a divorce law firm, you can also rate yourself on how well you can explain the process of getting a divorce in your state and connect the potential new customer to their local court. This will help ensure that your team provides an accurate and thorough explanation of the expectations during each call.

Don't forget to assess each call's overall customer satisfaction rating. This will enable you to measure how well you informed the potential new customers, helped them, and assured them they could get what they needed from your team. It may also help to track customer satisfaction over time so that you can identify any areas where improvement is required.

The scorecard should be an ongoing process, allowing for continuous improvement of your law firm's performance. Make sure to review all calls, if possible, or at least a random selection of calls if the volume is too high. But you do ideally want to audit every call.

Auditing your phone calls using a scorecard system is a powerful tool for improving sales effectiveness in law firms. By consistently rating key factors such as greeting effectiveness, qualification skills, empathy, name usage, reassurance, contact information gathering, appointment scheduling, value establishment, team positivity, and assumptive selling, you gain valuable insights into areas for improvement. Use these insights to refine your approach, enhance your communication skills, and increase your conversion rates. Remember, the audit process is ongoing, and continuous self-assessment is critical to continued growth and success in law firm sales.

# Take Action Based On How Well You Hit Your Numbers

Each time you look at your numbers, you should get insights into areas where you can improve. If you are not increasing your sign-up rate but are scoring well in your scorecard audits of the calls, there may be an issue with the quality of the leads. Explore ways to improve your marketing messaging and targeting.

If you are getting reasonably good conversion rates but still not meeting your target numbers, you may need to focus on the quality of the leads. Look at how well you connect with potential customers and assess if there is room for improvement in communication or empathy.

On the other hand, if your numbers are low overall, consider examining the sales process from top to bottom. If you are not successfully establishing value on the calls or achieving positive outcomes, then there may be an issue with your sales process. Take action and assess what needs to change to increase your conversion rates.

You should also examine other factors affecting your ability to convert potential customers into paying clients. Sometimes you may benefit from individualized coaching from an expert who can help

## CONNECT & CONVERT ACTIVITY

## Measuring Your Way to Success

*Complete this activity with the free worksheet from the Marketing Boss App Connect Convert Resource Library.*

Track the number of connections and conversions you make each day. Keeping a record of these achievements can make the process more enjoyable, as it enables you to celebrate every day you surpass your personal best and explore ways to refine your approach when you don't. Additionally, consider how your personal best contributes to the law firm's overarching goals. Reflecting on how your individual efforts align with and advance the firm's objectives can provide further motivation and offer clearer direction for your daily activities.

you with specific issues. If you struggle to overcome objections, working with a sales coach one-on-one can help you improve your skills. If you are struggling with limiting beliefs or other mindset issues, a mindset coach may benefit you.

Review the areas of this book as needed until these best practices come naturally and effortlessly. The more you practice, the better you will become at selling.

# CHAPTER 14

# Embrace The Journey

Congratulations on reading the best practices for creating meaningful connections with your law firm's potential clients. By now, you've analyzed the intricacies of law firm sales and absorbed invaluable insights about people's thoughts and feelings so you can best connect with them. But remember, this isn't the end. It's just the beginning of a transformative journey to developing habits that will allow you to connect with potential new customers in meaningful ways.

## Apply What You Learned

As you apply your new knowledge, embrace your firm's uniqueness and infuse your approach with a genuine touch that resonates with your audience. Some new tactics may initially feel awkward, so be patient with yourself. Fine-tune your strategies and watch as your connections deepen and your impact grows. Have faith in the process. With practice, you'll create lasting relationships with potential clients and expand opportunities for your firm.

Remember everything you've learned about building trustworthiness, creating meaningful connections, and showcasing why your firm is the perfect choice. Authenticity is key. Your potential new customers are looking for an honest, reliable law firm that's genuinely invested in their success, and you can offer just that.

Be bold and confident when you speak about your firm's values and beliefs, especially those you are most inspired by. Don't be afraid to share the unique aspects of your business that make it stand out from the crowd. This will help you continue cultivating meaningful connections. In this dynamic landscape, authenticity is your greatest asset and is pivotal to forging lasting relationships. Your practice will flourish with every genuine connection you make.

## Think Bigger Than Your Job

Consider how the skills from this book can help you achieve your job at the firm and your life goals. As you interact with others outside your work environment, get excited about testing your skills daily. Practice overcoming limiting beliefs, showing empathy, and defying objections in everyday scenarios. Your law firm will grow as you do.

Remember that knowledge is power. It will make your life easier and give you the confidence to go after bigger and better opportunities. Use the insights gleaned from this book to become a master communicator in all aspects of your life.

Strive to keep learning, adapting, and building meaningful connections that define your success. Your journey continues. Embrace it confidently and commit to making a difference. Enjoy the journey as you become a master at connecting with potential new clients and signing up cases like a boss!

# CHAPTER 15

# Qualifying Cases by Case Type

In previous chapters, we focused on strategies to connect. In this chapter, we will discuss qualifying cases based on the case types that your law firm handles. You will find a summary of some of the most common cases handled by law firms in the United States, along with an overview of what most law firms would consider a qualified lead for each respective case type. You will also see some suggested questions that you can ask to gather key information from prospects depending on the case type they describe.

Before you use these tips, make sure you have consulted your law firm for a list of matter types or case types that they consider ideal, as well as any unique qualifications they may have based on local laws, jurisdiction, and preferences.

Consider geography. Some law firms practice some or all of their matter types anywhere in the country, while others may be limited to a specific geography for some or all case types. For example, you may be an immigration law firm that handles cases around the country except for juvenile visa cases, where you may be limited to a specific state. Make sure you know what sort of cases your firm handles and in what areas so you can add qualifying questions accordingly.

As you qualify leads by case type and talk to potential new customers, understand they may also be anxious to get their answers. They may ask you for legal advice or pressure you to tell them if they have a strong case. If you are not an attorney, please politely explain that you are asking questions to gather initial information for your legal team to review. Explain that your goal is to provide a preliminary screening based on their answers to your questions so the legal team can review the details and provide qualified legal guidance later.

In most instances, you can answer questions as long as you explain that you are not giving them legal advice. Provide helpful information while staying compliant with legal and ethical obligations by answering questions within the scope of your role as a receptionist or intake professional. You can guide potential clients toward seeking the appropriate legal counsel from qualified attorneys who can provide accurate legal advice tailored to their needs.

Aside from being unethical for a nonattorney to give legal advice, there are some additional risks to consider. Providing legal advice without the proper qualifications and license is considered an unauthorized practice of law, which most jurisdictions prohibit. Somebody could hold you liable for any damages that result. If you knowingly or unknowingly give incorrect or misleading legal advice, it can lead to severe consequences for both the individual seeking advice and the law firm. By explicitly stating that you are not providing legal advice, you can help mitigate potential liability risks. This process safeguards the interests and rights of clients by ensuring they receive advice from professionals who can provide appropriate legal services.

If you are an attorney, refrain from giving legal advice if you realize that your client or potential new client is inquiring about

**CONNECT & CONVERT ACTIVITY**

## Qualifying Questions Roadmap

*Complete this activity with the free worksheet from the Marketing Boss App Connect Convert Resource Library.*

Review the qualifying questions for cases by case type outlined below for cases that your law firm handles. Then take it a step further by crafting a personalized list of questions that align with your specific law firm, by practice area using the suggested questions as inspiration. This exercise will enhance your client interactions and refine your approach qualifying leads that you can convert to loyal clients!

a legal matter outside your expertise. Attorneys are bound by ethical rules and guidelines that govern their practice, which protects consumers. You can explain this to clients and potential new clients as a standard of care you are taking to avoid any conflicts or violations that may arise from providing inaccurate or unqualified advice.

## Bankruptcy Law

A bankruptcy law case involves the legal process where individuals or businesses who cannot pay their debts seek relief from their financial obligations. Understanding the basics of bankruptcy law and the different case types within bankruptcy can help you effectively qualify leads for these cases.

The various case types under bankruptcy are listed below. However, as you discuss this type of matter with a potential new customer, you can consider some common factors that can generally affect the strength of a possible bankruptcy law case. These include the following.

**Financial Situation:** Determine if the individual or business is facing overwhelming debt and unable to make payments.

**Income and Assets:** Assess the income and asset profile to determine eligibility for specific bankruptcy chapters.

**Debt Types:** Analyze the nature of the debt, including consumer debt, business debt, tax debt, or medical debt.

**Legal Considerations:** Identify any potential legal issues or complications that may affect their eligibility for a bankruptcy filing.

Gathering the details of the matter from potential new customers may help emphasize how your legal team can likely help them.

**Evaluate Eligibility:** Determine the most appropriate bankruptcy chapter based on the unique circumstances of the individual or business.

**Assess Debt Relief Options:** Explore alternatives to bankruptcy, such as debt consolidation or negotiation.

**Provide Legal Guidance:** Advise the client on the necessary documentation, filing procedures, and legal requirements for a successful bankruptcy case.

Note that several bankruptcy chapters serve different purposes depending on the type of debtor and the desired outcome. The following is a summary of the most common chapters.

**Chapter 7:** Also known as "liquidation bankruptcy," Chapter 7 is available to individuals, businesses, and partnerships. It involves the sale of non-exempt assets to repay creditors. Any remaining eligible debts are typically discharged.

**Chapter 11:** Primarily used by businesses, Chapter 11 allows for reorganizing or restructuring debts while the company continues its operations. It provides an opportunity to develop a repayment plan and regain financial stability.

**Chapter 12:** Specifically designed for family farmers and fishermen, Chapter 12 bankruptcy provides a repayment plan tailored to their unique circumstances. It allows them to restructure debt and continue their agricultural or fishing operations.

**Chapter 13:** Referred to as "reorganization bankruptcy," Chapter 13 is available to individuals with regular income who want to create a manageable repayment plan to satisfy their debts over three to five years.

**Chapter 15:** This chapter deals with cross-border bankruptcies and provides a framework for cooperation between the U.S. and foreign courts to handle cases involving debtors, assets, or claims in multiple countries.

## Individual Bankruptcy

A good case for a lawyer who handles individual bankruptcy cases is typically one where an individual is eligible for bankruptcy relief. Gather information about the severity of their financial hardships, the debt amounts and types, income and expenses, and information that will help your law firm determine what bankruptcy chapter they need.

Ask the following questions to gather essential information to determine if a potential client may meet the qualifications for an individual bankruptcy case.

1. Are you struggling with overwhelming debt you cannot repay?
2. Have you experienced a significant decrease in income or faced unexpected financial challenges?
3. How much debt do you currently owe? (e.g., credit cards, medical bills, personal loans, etc.)
4. Do you have both secured and unsecured debts? (e.g., mortgage, car loan, student loans)
5. Are you being pursued by creditors or facing potential legal actions such as lawsuits or wage garnishments?
6. What is your current income level? Is it insufficient to cover your monthly expenses and debt payments?
7. Do you need help to make minimum payments on your debts or to keep from falling behind on bills?
8. Do you have substantial assets at risk in a bankruptcy proceeding? (e.g., valuable real estate, investments)
9. Are most of your assets exempt from seizure under bankruptcy laws? (e.g., basic household items, personal vehicle)
10. Have you explored other alternatives to bankruptcy, such as debt consolidation or negotiation?
11. Given your financial circumstances, how confident are you in repaying your debts?
12. Are you aware of the different types of bankruptcy chapters, such as Chapter 7 and Chapter 13?
13. Do you prefer a particular bankruptcy chapter based on your situation and goals?
14. Have you recently transferred any property or assets that may raise concerns in a bankruptcy filing?
15. Are you facing any legal challenges or potential disputes related to your debts?

# Business Bankruptcy

If the potential new client is calling on behalf of a business, you can explore qualifying them for a business bankruptcy case. There are questions you can use to assess a business's eligibility for bankruptcy relief based on the level of financial distress, debt amounts and types, viability of the business, legal actions, cash flow and profitability, assets and liabilities, business structure, and more.

The following are some questions you can ask to gather crucial information to assess if a potential client has a valid case for business bankruptcy.

1. Is the business facing overwhelming debt that it cannot repay?
2. Has the business experienced a significant decrease in revenue or faced unexpected financial challenges?
3. How much debt does the business currently owe? (e.g., loans, credit lines, trade payables)
4. Are there both secured and unsecured debts? (e.g., mortgages, equipment financing, vendor payments)
5. Is the business still operational or on the verge of shutting down?
6. Can the business recover and become financially viable with proper restructuring?
7. Are there pending lawsuits, foreclosures, or creditor collection efforts against the business?
8. Has the business received any legal notices or demands from creditors?
9. Is the business generating enough cash to cover its operational expenses and debt obligations?
10. Has the business been consistently profitable, or has it been experiencing losses?
11. What assets does the business possess? (e.g., real estate, equipment, inventory)
12. Are there any significant or contingent liabilities the business needs to address?
13. Is the business a sole proprietorship, partnership, corporation, or legal entity?
14. How would bankruptcy affect the owners' liability for business debts?

15. Have other alternatives to bankruptcy, such as debt restructuring or negotiation, been explored?
16. What efforts have been made to secure additional financing or investment for the business?

## Creditors' Rights

If the potential new client mentions they are a creditor, you may want to explore a line of questions that can help determine if they qualify for a creditor's rights case. In these cases, creditors can seek legal protections and remedies in bankruptcy proceedings.

The following are some questions you can ask to gather essential information to determine if a potential client may meet the qualifications for a creditor's rights case.

1. How much debt is owed to your organization by the debtor?
2. Has the debtor failed to make payments or defaulted on the debt?
3. Does any collateral secure the debt? If so, what type of collateral is involved?
4. Is the debt unsecured, such as credit card debt or unpaid invoices?
5. Do you have written agreements, contracts, or promissory notes outlining the terms of the debt and the debtor's obligations?
6. Have you adequately filed any necessary liens against the debtor's assets?
7. Have you attempted to communicate with the debtor regarding the outstanding debt?
8. Have you sent the debtor any demand letters or notices of default?
9. Has the debtor acknowledged their default on the debt?
10. Have you taken any legal actions to enforce the debt, such as filing a lawsuit or obtaining a judgment?
11. Are you aware if the debtor has filed for bankruptcy protection?
12. If so, which chapter of bankruptcy was filed?
13. Have you taken steps to protect and preserve your rights as a creditor in the event of a bankruptcy filing?
14. Are you familiar with the automatic stay provisions in bankruptcy that temporarily halt collection efforts?

15. What are your expectations regarding recovering the outstanding debt in a bankruptcy proceeding?
16. Are you aware of any specific assets or sources of potential recovery?

## Corporate Law

The corporate law practice area deals with legal matters related to corporations and other business entities. It encompasses various legal services that assist businesses in their formation, governance, compliance, transactions, and general operations. Potential new clients who need a corporate law attorney are generally looking for deep knowledge and expertise in the specific practice area they need, which can include company formation, governance, regulatory compliance, mergers and acquisitions, contracts, and intellectual property. An excellent corporate law attorney also understands the business context in which legal matters arise. They grasp the underlying commercial considerations and align legal strategies with business objectives.

### Business Formation

Business formation cases involve assisting clients in choosing the appropriate legal structure for their business, such as forming a corporation, limited liability company (LLC), partnership, or sole proprietorship. If the potential new customer mentions wanting to start a new business or restructure their existing business entity, they may have a business formation case.

Ideal clients have a clear and well-defined purpose. The client should have a specific business idea or objective, such as starting a new company, expanding an existing business, or restructuring their business entity. They should also commit to complying with the legal requirements of forming a business entity, including fulfilling state-specific registration, licensing, and fulfilling regulatory obligations.

Clients seeking business formation assistance often want liability protection. An ideal client will likely understand the importance of establishing a separate legal entity (such as a corporation or LLC) to shield personal assets from business liabilities.

Note it if the potential new client mentions a more complex ownership structure, such as multiple shareholders or partners. They may need additional legal guidance. Clients with intricate ownership arrangements may benefit the most from the expertise of a business formation attorney.

Potential new clients for this case type may also ask about customized legal documents, such as articles of incorporation, bylaws, operating agreements, or partnership agreements. This inquiry can indicate a good case for a lawyer specializing in business formation.

The following are some questions you can ask to gather essential information to determine if a potential client may be an ideal candidate for a business formation case.

1. What is your business idea or objective? Are you looking to start a new business or restructure an existing one?
2. Do you know the legal requirements for forming a business entity in your state? If so, are you prepared to fulfill those obligations?
3. Are you seeking liability protection for your assets? Do you understand the benefits of establishing a separate legal entity?
4. Does your business involve a complex ownership structure? Are there multiple shareholders or partners involved?
5. Do you need customized legal documents specific to your business, such as articles of incorporation, bylaws, operating agreements, or partnership agreements?

## Corporate Governance

A corporate governance case refers to a legal matter or dispute related to corporations' governing and oversight practices. It involves issues concerning the rights, responsibilities, and relationships between different stakeholders within a company, including shareholders, board members, executives, and other parties involved in corporate decision-making. Suppose a potential new customer mentions board of director duties, shareholder rights, executive compensation, insider trading and market manipulation, disclosure and financial reporting, mergers and acquisitions, shareholder activism, and regulatory compliance. In that case, you can ask questions to qualify them as a corporate governance lead.

Remember that a strong case for corporate governance may involve allegations of breaches of fiduciary duties by board members or executives, such as conflicts of interest, self-dealing, lack of independence, or failure to act in the company's and its shareholders' best interests.

Some cases may involve significant impacts on shareholder rights, such as denial of voting rights, inadequate disclosure of material information, unfair treatment of shareholders, or actions that dilute shareholder value, which have a stronger basis for legal action. In other cases, there may be evidence of violations of securities laws, accounting standards, or other relevant regulations related to corporate governance practices that can provide a solid foundation for legal action.

If shareholders suffer demonstrable financial harm due to alleged corporate governance issues, such as a decline in stock value, loss of investment opportunities, or improper distribution of dividends, that can also strengthen a case. Cases that involve reputational damage to the company due to corporate governance failures, which may affect investor confidence, stakeholder relationships, or public perception, can be influential in pursuing legal remedies.

The following are some questions you can ask to gather essential information to determine if a potential client may be an ideal candidate for a corporate governance case.

1. Are you aware of any specific instances where board members or executives may have engaged in actions that conflict with their fiduciary duties or failed to act in the best interests of the company and its shareholders?
2. Have there been any notable violations of shareholder rights, such as denial of voting rights, inadequate disclosure, unfair treatment, or actions that have negatively impacted shareholder value?
3. Are there any indications or evidence that the company has violated securities laws, accounting standards, or other regulatory requirements related to corporate governance practices?
4. Have shareholders experienced financial harm due to alleged corporate governance issues, such as declining stock value or losing investment opportunities?

5. Has the company's reputation been adversely affected due to potential corporate governance failures, leading to concerns about the corporations' investor confidence or stakeholder relationships?

## Contracts and Commercial Transactions

Contracts and commercial transactions encompass legally binding agreements and business dealings between parties. They can involve purchasing or selling goods, services, or property, lease supplements, licensing agreements, joint ventures, or other contractual arrangements. Your firm may handle some or all of these contracts and commercial transaction case types.

**Breach of Contract:** A strong case may involve a clear breach of contract, where one party fails to fulfill their obligations as specified in the agreement. This could include non-payment, non-delivery of goods or services, or failure to meet other contractual terms.

**Disputes over Contract Interpretation:** Cases where the parties have conflicting interpretations of contract terms or clauses, leading to disagreements or conflicts regarding the rights and obligations of each party.

**Fraud or Misrepresentation:** If one party engaged in fraudulent activities or made false representations during contract formation, resulting in harm or damages to the other party, it can provide grounds for legal action.

**Unfair Business Practices:** Cases involving unfair or deceptive business practices, such as antitrust violations, price-fixing, monopolistic behavior, or other actions that harm competition or consumers.

**Noncompliance with Regulatory Requirements:** Cases where one party fails to comply with legal or regulatory requirements related to the specific industry or transaction, which may result in violations of applicable laws or regulations.

**Unilateral Termination or Modification:** Instances where one party unilaterally terminates or modifies the contract without proper justification or compliance with contractual provisions, leading to disputes or damages for the other party.

To determine if a potential client may have a valid case in contracts and commercial transactions, the following are some questions you can ask.

1. Is there a written contract governing the transaction or business relationship?
2. Has either party failed to fulfill their obligations as specified in the contract?
3. Are there any disputes or disagreements regarding interpreting contract terms or clauses?
4. Have you been subjected to fraudulent activities or misrepresentations during the negotiation or execution of the contract?
5. Are there any unfair business practices or antitrust concerns related to the transaction?
6. Has either party failed to comply with legal or regulatory requirements relevant to the specific industry or transaction?
7. Has one party unilaterally terminated or modified the contract without proper justification or compliance with contractual provisions?

## Regulatory Compliance

Regulatory compliance refers to the adherence and conformity to laws, rules, regulations, and standards set by government bodies or industry-specific authorities. A regulatory compliance case typically arises when a company or individual is accused of violating these regulations or failing to meet the required standards.

Listen for the following topics.

**Regulatory Violations:** A strong case may involve clear evidence of violations or non-compliance with specific regulations applicable to the industry or sector. This can include failure to obtain necessary permits or licenses, improper handling or disposal of hazardous substances, or non-adherence to safety protocols.

**Legal Consequences:** These are cases where the alleged regulatory violations have resulted in actual harm, damage, or risk to public health, safety, or the environment and tend to have stronger legal foundations. This could involve product recalls, workplace accidents, or environmental pollution.

**Documentation and Recordkeeping:** Cases where there is a lack of proper documentation, recordkeeping, or internal control mechanisms to demonstrate compliance with regulatory requirements can strengthen the argument for regulatory violations.

**Whistleblower Complaints:** These cases are based on whistleblower complaints or reports from employees, customers, or other individuals who have direct knowledge of the alleged regulatory violations and can provide substantial evidence to support the legal claims.

**Pattern of Noncompliance:** A history of repeated or ongoing noncompliance with regulatory requirements can demonstrate a systematic failure to meet the necessary standards and strengthen the case against the accused party.

To determine if a potential client may have a valid regulatory compliance case, the following are some questions you can ask.

1. Are you aware of any specific regulations or standards that your company or individuals within your organization must comply with?
2. Have there been any instances where your company has been accused of or cited for violating regulatory requirements?
3. Has the alleged noncompliance resulted in any actual harm, damage, or risk to public health, safety, or the environment?
4. Are there any documented instances or reports from employees or other individuals raising concerns about potential regulatory violations?
5. Is there a pattern of noncompliance or repeated failure to meet regulatory standards within your organization?

## Mergers and Acquisitions

If a potential new customer is inquiring about the consolidation or combination of two or more companies through a merger, acquisition, or other similar transactions, they may be a candidate for a mergers and acquisition (M&A) case. It typically involves the transfer of ownership, assets, and liabilities between the involved parties.

In a M&A case, one company may acquire another, or two companies may merge to form a new entity. The purpose of such transactions can vary and may include strategic expansion, market consolidation, diversification, or gaining access to new technologies or markets.

They will likely need a lawyer who handles M&A to guide them through the process, ensure compliance with relevant laws and regulations, protect their client's interests, and facilitate a successful transaction. A M&A lawyer assists in structuring the deal, conducting legal and due diligence, negotiating and documenting the transaction terms, and providing advice on regulatory matters and potential risks.

The following are some terms you may hear and what they mean.

**Antitrust Compliance:** These are cases where a proposed transaction may raise antitrust concerns due to potential market concentration or an adverse impact on competition. This could involve an analysis of market share, competitive effects, and potential regulatory scrutiny.

**Due Diligence:** A strong case often involves comprehensive due diligence conducted by the buyer or seller to identify potential risks, liabilities, or material information that may impact the transaction. Failure to disclose relevant information can be grounds for legal action.

**Breach of Contract:** Cases where one party fails to fulfill its obligations as outlined in the merger or acquisition agreement fall under breach of contract. This could include nonpayment, failure to transfer assets or shares, or violating noncompete clauses.

**Misrepresentation or Fraud:** If one party engages in fraudulent activities or makes false representations during the negotiation or execution of the deal, it can provide grounds for legal action. This could include misrepresenting financial statements, undisclosed liabilities, or intentionally omitting material facts.

**Shareholder Rights:** These are cases where shareholders' rights have been infringed upon, such as minority shareholders being unfairly treated or excluded from decision-making processes during the M&A transaction.

**Regulatory Compliance:** Cases involving noncompliance with relevant laws, regulations, or industry-specific requirements governing mergers and acquisitions. This could include failure to obtain necessary approvals or licenses from regulatory authorities.

The following are some questions you can ask to assess a M&A case.

1. Are you currently involved in or considering a merger, acquisition, joint venture, or any other type of corporate transaction?
2. Have you performed due diligence to assess the potential risks, liabilities, or material information related to the transaction?
3. Are there any concerns about antitrust compliance or potential regulatory scrutiny?
4. Has either party failed to fulfill its obligations outlined in the merger or acquisition agreement?
5. Are there any allegations of misrepresentation, fraud, or intentional omissions of material facts during the deal negotiation or execution?
6. Have shareholders' rights been infringed upon or compromised during the M&A process?
7. Have you ensured compliance with all relevant laws, regulations, and industry-specific requirements governing mergers and acquisitions?
8. What is the strategic objective behind the proposed merger or acquisition?
9. Can clear synergies or growth opportunities be achieved through the transaction?
10. Are both parties financially stable and capable of supporting the transaction?
11. Have financial statements and projections been prepared to assess the economic feasibility of the deal?
12. Have any legal or regulatory issues been identified that could affect the proposed transaction?

13. Is the industry subject to specific regulations that need to be considered?
14. Has comprehensive due diligence been conducted on the target company, including its financials, contracts, intellectual property, and potential liabilities?
15. Are there any red flags or concerns arising from the due diligence process?
16. Has the valuation of the target company or assets been determined, and are both parties in agreement with the assessment?
17. What are the proposed terms of the transaction, such as purchase price, payment structure, and any contingencies?
18. How will the transaction be financed? Are there sufficient funds or access to financing to complete the deal?
19. Have discussions with potential lenders or investors taken place?
20. Have the necessary approvals been obtained from shareholders and the board of directors?
21. Are there any significant stakeholders or key individuals who need to be involved in the decision-making process?
22. Has a plan for post-merger integration been developed to ensure a smooth transition and maximize synergies?
23. What are the potential challenges or risks associated with integrating the two companies?

## Securities Regulation

Securities regulation refers to the body of laws and regulations that govern the issuance, sale, and trading of securities, including stocks, bonds, and other investment instruments. A securities regulation case typically arises when there are allegations or violations of these laws and regulations.

A potential new client with a securities regulation case may mention some or all of the following issues.

**Securities Fraud:** A strong case may involve allegations of fraudulent activities related to selling or trading securities. This could include misrepresentation of information, insider trading, market manipulation, or Ponzi schemes.

**Nondisclosure or Misleading Statements:** Cases with evidence of nondisclosure or misleading statements in offering documents, financial statements, or other materials provided to investors can strengthen the argument for securities fraud.

**Regulatory Violations:** Cases where companies or individuals fail to comply with specific securities laws and regulations, such as registration requirements, reporting obligations, or anti-fraud provisions fall under regulatory violations. This could involve violations of the Securities Act of 1933, the Securities Exchange Act of 1934, or other relevant laws and regulations.

**Investor Harm or Losses:** If investors have suffered financial harm or losses due to the alleged securities violations, it can provide grounds for legal action. This could involve monetary damages, loss of investments, or diminished value of securities.

**Materiality of Information:** Cases where the alleged violation involves material information that could have influenced an investor's decision-making process fall under this category. Materiality is information that reasonably impacts an investor's judgment regarding the security being offered or traded.

To determine if a potential client may have a valid securities regulation case, the following are some questions you can ask.

1. Have you invested in securities such as stocks, bonds, or other investment instruments?
2. Are you aware of any allegations or suspicions of fraudulent activities related to your investments?
3. Have you encountered nondisclosure or misleading statements in offering documents or financial statements?
4. Do you suspect any securities laws and regulations violations by the involved parties?
5. Have you suffered financial harm or losses due to these alleged violations?
6. Is there any material information that was not properly disclosed and could have influenced your investment decisions?

## Contract Drafting and Negotiation

In contract drafting and negotiation cases, potential new customers may need help with creating, interpreting, or enforcing contracts. This area of law focuses on ensuring that contracts are legally sound, clearly drafted, and aligned with the parties' intentions.

Listen for qualities that make up a strong case, such as the following.

**Ambiguity or Vagueness:** A strong case may involve contracts that contain ambiguous or vague language, leading to confusion or disagreement among the parties about the terms or obligations, resulting in the need for interpretation or renegotiation.

**Breach of Contract:** Cases where one party fails to fulfill their obligations as outlined in the contract fall under breach of contract. This could include nonperformance, delayed performance, or failure to adhere to specific terms or conditions.

**Invalid or Unenforceable Provisions**: Cases where certain provisions within the contract are deemed invalid or unenforceable due to legal deficiencies, lack of consideration, violation of public policy, or other reasons fall into this category..

**Misrepresentation or Fraud:** If one party engages in fraudulent activities or makes false representations during the contract negotiation or drafting process, it can provide grounds for legal action.

**Dispute Resolution Mechanisms:** Cases involving disputes over the interpretation or implementation of dispute resolution mechanisms outlined in the contract, such as arbitration or mediation clauses, fall into this category.

You can ask questions like the following to determine if the potential new customer has a contract drafting and negotiation case.

1. Do you need assistance drafting or negotiating a contract?
2. Have you or others entered into a contract or agreement with another party?
3. Are any provisions within the contract unclear or open to interpretation?

4. Has either party failed to fulfill the obligations outlined in the contract?
5. Are there any provisions within the contract that could be deemed invalid or unenforceable to your knowledge?
6. As far as you know, were there any misrepresentations or fraudulent activities by the other party during the negotiation or drafting process?
7. Are you experiencing a dispute related to the interpretation or implementation of dispute resolution mechanisms outlined in the contract?

## Corporate Restructuring and Insolvency

Corporate restructuring and insolvency legal services involve assisting businesses facing financial distress, bankruptcy, or insolvency issues. This area of law focuses on finding solutions to help companies reorganize, repay debts, and navigate the complex legal processes involved in corporate restructuring or insolvency proceedings. A potential new customer with a corporate restructuring and insolvency case may talk about the following topics.

**Financial Distress:** A company experiencing significant financial difficulties, such as mounting debt, liquidity problems, declining revenues, or an inability to meet financial obligations, may be a candidate for corporate restructuring or insolvency.

**Bankruptcy or Insolvency Filing:** A company may be considering or has already filed for bankruptcy or insolvency protection. This could include Chapter 7, Chapter 11, or Chapter 13 bankruptcy filings under the U.S. Bankruptcy Code.

**Creditor or Debtor Rights:** There may be disputes or negotiations between creditors and debtors regarding debt repayment, asset liquidation, restructuring plans, or other matters related to insolvency proceedings.

**Restructuring Strategies:** They may ask for help from a lawyer who can develop and implement effective restructuring strategies to help the company reorganize its operations, renegotiate debt terms, or pursue alternative financing options.

**Avoidance Actions:** Cases involving the identification and pursuit of avoidance actions, such as preferences or fraudulent transfers, to recover assets for the benefit of creditors, fall into this category.

To determine if a potential client may have a valid corporate restructuring and insolvency case, the following are some questions you can ask.

1. Is your company facing significant financial challenges or distress?
2. Have you considered or already filed for bankruptcy or insolvency protection?
3. Are you experiencing disputes with creditors or debtors regarding debt repayment or other financial obligations?
4. Are you seeking assistance in developing and implementing a restructuring plan for your company?
5. Have you identified any potential avoidance actions that could help recover assets for the benefit of creditors?

## Employment Law

An employment law case involves legal matters related to the relationship between employers and employees but does not necessarily include personal injuries in the workplace. Many law firm prospects mistakenly label personal injury cases as employment law cases and vice versa. It is a perfect example of why it's important to have potential new customers describe their legal matters rather than relying on them to tell you what sort of case they think they have.

While worker's compensation concerns personal injuries in the workplace, employment law cases cover other issues between employees and employers. For instance, an employer failing to compensate an employee for a reason other than a work injury can fall into the employment law category. Employment law cases can encompass wrongful termination, discrimination, harassment, wage and hour disputes, workplace safety violations, and retaliation. Gather essential information to help determine if the potential client's case falls within the scope of employment law and whether your firm can provide the necessary legal services.

The following are some qualifying questions you can ask.

1. Are you seeking legal assistance for an employment-related issue such as wrongful termination, discrimination, or wage disputes?
2. Have you taken any initial steps to address the issue, such as filing a complaint with your employer or a government agency?
3. What evidence or documentation do you have to support your claim? This may include emails, performance reviews, pay stubs, or witness statements.
4. Is there a specific timeline for your case, such as impending deadlines or upcoming hearings?
5. Have you consulted with any other attorneys or legal professionals regarding this matter?
6. Have you experienced any negative consequences or retaliation for raising concerns about your employment?

## Discrimination Claims

Discrimination claims cases should have strong evidence, clear violations of anti-discrimination laws, and potential for substantial damages or remedies. Let's consider an age discrimination case to provide a more specific example. Remember that you can use a similar approach and line of questioning to qualify racial discrimination cases, sexual harassment cases, or other discrimination cases.

## Age Discrimination Case

An age discrimination case involves individuals believing they have been mistreated or discriminated against based on age. The following are some factors that make a strong age discrimination case.

**Direct Evidence:** Strong evidence that directly shows discriminatory intent is crucial, including explicit statements or actions indicating bias against older individuals.

**Adverse Employment Action:** The plaintiff must show that they suffered an adverse employment action due to discrimination such as demotion, termination, denial of promotion, or unequal treatment compared to younger employees.

**Comparative Evidence:** A comparison between the treatment of the plaintiff and that of younger employees in similar circumstances can help establish the presence of age-based discrimination.

**Pattern of Discrimination:** Evidence of a consistent pattern of discriminatory behavior within the company or organization strengthens the case. This can involve multiple instances of age-based mistreatment or a pervasive culture of age bias.

**Pretext:** Demonstrating that the employer's stated reasons for the adverse action were a pretext to cover up age discrimination is important. This can involve showing inconsistencies, contradictions, or lack of credibility in the employer's explanation.

The following are some suggested questions you can ask to uncover qualifiers for a strong age discrimination case.

1. Have you experienced any adverse employment actions, such as demotion, termination, or denial of promotions that you believe may be related to your age?
2. Can you provide specific instances where you felt you were treated differently or less favorably than younger colleagues?
3. Are there any documented or witnessed instances where superiors, colleagues, or management expressed age-related comments or bias?
4. Have you observed a pattern of similar mistreatment or discrimination against other older employees in your workplace?
5. Were the reasons given by your employer for the adverse action consistent, credible, and supported by evidence?

## Harassment Claims

A harassment claims case refers to legal action taken by individuals who have experienced unwanted and offensive behavior in the workplace that creates a hostile or intimidating environment. Harassment behavior includes characteristics such as race, color, religion, sex, national origin, age, disability, or genetic information.

The following are some key aspects of a harassment claims case.

**Unwelcome Conduct:** The behavior must be unwelcome and unsolicited by the individual who experienced it. It can include offensive comments, slurs, derogatory jokes, physical contact, or inappropriate behavior.

**Protected Characteristic:** The harassment must link to a protected characteristic recognized under federal or state laws. This means the behavior targets an individual based on their race, gender, religion, or other protected attribute.

**Hostile Work Environment:** A strong case involves proving that the conduct created a hostile work environment. This requires demonstrating that the behavior was severe or pervasive enough to create an intimidating, abusive, or offensive atmosphere that interferes with an individual's ability to work.

**Employer Liability:** Employers can be held responsible for harassment by supervisors, managers, or coworkers. They may also be liable for harassment by nonemployees, such as clients or customers if they knew about the conduct and failed to take appropriate action to address it.

**Reporting and Documentation:** Individuals who experience harassment should report the incidents to their employer or follow the company's reporting procedures. Documentation such as emails, texts, or witness statements can strengthen the case and establish a pattern of behavior.

Suggested questions to qualify a harassment claim include the following.

1. Can you describe the specific incidents or behaviors that you believe constitute harassment in your workplace?
2. Have you reported the harassment to your employer or followed the company's reporting procedures? If yes, what actions have employers taken in response?
3. How has harassment affected your ability to work or created a hostile environment?
4. Do you have any evidence or documentation, such as emails, texts, or witness statements that support your allegations?
5. Are there any policies or practices within your company that contribute to or enable the harassment to occur?

# Wrongful Termination

Wrongful termination cases include cases with clear evidence of unlawful termination based on discrimination, retaliation, breach of contract, or violation of public policy. There has to be a violation of rights that are legally defined and protected rights. When an employee believes that their dismissal from employment was illegal or in violation of their rights, they may discuss some of the following as they describe their legal matter.

**Discrimination:** If an employee is fired based on protected characteristics such as race, color, religion, sex, national origin, age, disability, or genetic information, it may constitute wrongful termination.

**Retaliation:** If an employer terminates an employee in response to the employee engaging in legally protected activities, such as reporting harassment, discrimination, or illegal practices, it may be wrongful termination.

**Breach of Contract**: If an enforceable employment contract outlines employment terms and conditions and the employer violates those terms by terminating the employee without cause, it may be considered wrongful termination.

**Violation of Public Policy**: If an employer fires the employee for reasons that violate established public policy, such as being terminated for refusing to engage in illegal activities or exercising their legal rights, it may be wrongful termination.

**Constructive Dismissal:** In certain cases, an employee may claim constructive dismissal if the working conditions become intolerable due to actions or behavior by the employer, forcing the employee to resign involuntarily.

Ask the following questions to gauge if a potential new customer may have a wrongful termination case.

1. Why do you believe your termination was wrongful? Can you provide specific details about any indications of discrimination, retaliation, breach of contract, or violation of public policy?

2. Do you have any evidence supporting your claim, such as emails, performance evaluations, witness statements, or documented incidents related to your termination?
3. Were there any explicit statements or actions by your employer or supervisors that suggest discriminatory or retaliatory motives for your termination?
4. Did you have an employment contract? If so, what were the terms and conditions outlined in the contract? How do you believe your employer breached them?
5. Were there any incidents or actions by your employer that created an intolerable work environment, leading to your resignation? Provide specific details and any documentation.

## Wage and Hour Disputes

If a potential new customer describes instances where there may have been violations of federal or state wage and hour laws, they may have a wage and hour case. A wage and hour dispute case refers to legal disputes between employees and employers concerning the payment of wages, hours worked, and overtime pay. These cases typically involve violations of laws such as the Fair Labor Standards Act (FLSA) at the federal level or similar state-specific labor laws. Common issues in these cases include the following.

**Minimum Wage Violations:** If an employer fails to pay employees the federal or state-mandated minimum wage, it may constitute a wage violation.

**Unpaid Wages:** When an employer withholds salary or fails to pay earned commissions, bonuses, or tips, it may be considered an unpaid wages violation.

**Overtime Pay:** If eligible employees work more than 40 hours in a work week but the employer doesn't compensate them at the legally required overtime rate—usually 1.5 times their regular pay rate—it may be an overtime pay violation.

**Employee Misclassification:** Employers may misclassify workers as independent contractors instead of employees to avoid providing benefits or paying overtime. If an individual is misclassified and should be classified as an employee, it may be a violation.

**Improper Deductions:** If an employer makes unauthorized deductions from an employee's wages, such as for breakages, uniforms, or cash register shortages, it may be a wage violation.

Ask the following questions to determine if a potential new customer has a wage and hour dispute case.

1. Have you experienced any issues related to paying your wages, such as unpaid wages, withheld commissions, or delayed payments?
2. Are you regularly working more than 40 hours a week without receiving overtime pay at the legally mandated rate?
3. Have you been classified as an independent contractor instead of an employee? Can you provide details about your job responsibilities and the level of control exerted by the employer over your work?
4. Have you noticed any unauthorized deductions from your wages, such as for breakages, uniforms, or other expenses?
5. Are you aware of any other employees within your organization facing similar wage and hour issues?

## Family Law

Familial law cases are usually related to marriage, divorce, child custody, adoption, domestic violence, paternity, and more. Note that there is also an area within immigration law that involves families that can, for example, include requests for citizenship through marriage. Still, those are considered immigration cases and not family law cases. True family law cases are centered around resolving conflicts and making decisions that affect the family unit and are unrelated to immigration.

The following are some qualifying questions you can use to gather insights about whether someone needs a family law attorney in general.

1. Are you seeking legal assistance for a divorce, child custody, adoption, or any other family-related matter?

2. Have you taken any legal steps, such as filing for divorce or obtaining a restraining order?
3. How long have you been facing this issue, and what efforts have you made to resolve it?
4. Are there any particular challenges or concerns regarding the case?
5. Do you have any documentation or evidence supporting your case?
6. Are there any time-sensitive factors involved, such as pending court dates or upcoming custody hearings?
7. Have you consulted with any other attorneys or legal professionals regarding this matter?
8. Are you aware of any specific state laws or regulations that may apply to your situation?

## Divorce

A divorce case centers on a married couple with clear grounds for divorce, which can include irreconcilable differences or other significant issues resolved by ending the union. A divorce case is also referred to as a dissolution of marriage. It is a legal process that ends the marital relationship between two individuals. It involves resolving various aspects related to the termination of the marriage, such as division of assets and debts, child custody and visitation, child support, alimony or spousal support, and any other matters specific to the couple's situation.

Characteristics that need a divorce lawyer include the following.

**Clear Grounds for Divorce:** In the United States, divorces are granted on either fault or no-fault grounds. A good case for a divorce lawyer may involve clear evidence of fault-based grounds, such as adultery, cruelty, abandonment, or imprisonment. No-fault divorces based on an irretrievable breakdown of the marriage or living apart for a certain period can also be strong cases.

**Significant Issues Needing Resolution**: A good divorce case often involves complex issues that require legal assistance. These may include the division of marital property, determining child custody and visitation schedules, calculating child support, and assessing the need for spousal support or alimony. The more substantial the issues, the more essential it becomes to seek help from an experienced attorney.

**Financial Complexity:** If the couple has substantial assets, investments, or business interests, it can complicate the divorce case. Matters like valuing and dividing these assets require specialized legal expertise. In some instances, concerns about the other spouse having hidden assets or engaging in financial misconduct may strengthen the case.

**Child-Related Issues:** When children are involved, determining child custody, visitation schedules, and calculating child support are critical aspects of a divorce case. Cases involving issues such as parental alienation, child abuse, or neglect require immediate legal intervention like emergency custody hearings or temporary protection orders (TPOs).

You can ask questions to assess if a potential client may have a valid divorce case, such as the following.

1. What are the reasons for seeking a divorce? Is there clear evidence of fault-based grounds, or have you been living apart for the required period for a no-fault divorce?
2. Can you provide an overview of the marital assets and debts you will divide? Are there significant financial complexities, such as complex investments or business interests?
3. Do you have children? How many, and what are their ages? Are there any existing custody arrangements? Are there concerns about the well-being of the children?
4. Are there any specific concerns regarding spousal support or alimony based on the financial situations of both parties?
5. Have there been any instances of domestic violence, abuse, or other significant challenges in the marriage?

## Child Custody and Support

A child custody and support case is a legal proceeding that addresses children's care, custody, and financial support when parents or guardians separate or divorce. The primary goal is to determine the child's best interests while establishing parenting arrangements and ensuring appropriate financial support from both parents. For instance, there may be a noncustodial parent with or without visitation rights, or both may have split custody. Based on that, the amount of child support can be calculated along with other factors like income, etc. Factors that affect this sort of case can include the following.

**Child's Best Interests:** A good child custody and support case focuses on the well-being and best interests of the child. The court will consider factors such as the child's age, emotional and physical needs, educational requirements, and any special considerations (e.g., medical conditions).

**Parental Fitness:** Cases concerning parental fitness, including factors like substance abuse, domestic violence, neglect, or criminal behavior, are stronger cases. You should inquire about any such concerns to assess the potential strength of the case.

**Primary Caregiver:** When determining child custody, courts often consider the primary caregiver, meaning the parent primarily responsible for the child's day-to-day care. If the potential client has been the primary caregiver, it strengthens their case for custody rights.

**Stability and Continuity:** Courts generally prioritize maintaining stability and continuity in the child's life. It can strengthen their case if the potential client can demonstrate a stable living environment, school attendance, community ties, and consistent involvement in the child's life.

**Financial Circumstances:** Child support cases involve assessing the financial circumstances of both parents and determining an appropriate amount of support for the child. A good case may involve significant financial disparities between the parents or concerns about the noncustodial parent's ability to provide adequate support.

To determine if a potential client may have a valid child custody and support case, you can ask the following questions.

1. Can you provide an overview of the current custody arrangement for your child? Are there any concerns about the child's safety or well-being with the other parent?
2. What is your role as the primary caregiver? How involved have you been in the child's day-to-day care and upbringing?
3. Are there any concerns about the other parent's fitness to care for the child, such as substance abuse, domestic violence, neglect, or criminal behavior?
4. Can you provide information about the child's living situation, school attendance, community involvement, and consistency of care?
5. Are there any significant financial disparities between you and the other parent? Do you believe the noncustodial parent could provide adequate financial support for the child?

## Adoption

An adoption case is a legal process where individuals or couples become the legal parents of a child who is not biologically their own. It is a significant and life-changing event that requires careful consideration and adherence to legal requirements. Adoptions can take various forms, including agency adoptions, private adoptions, domestic adoptions, or international adoptions.

A good adoption case involves factors contributing to a successful adoption process and ensuring the child's best interests. Common issues in these cases include the following.

**Eligibility and Preparedness:** Prospective adoptive parents must meet certain eligibility criteria, including age, marital status, and sometimes even residency requirements. A good case involves clients who meet these qualifications and have prepared themselves mentally, emotionally, and financially for adoption responsibilities.

**Legal Compliance:** Adoption cases require strict adherence to legal procedures, documentation, and regulations. A good case involves clients who have taken the necessary steps to comply with all legal requirements, such as background checks, home studies, and consent from birth parents or legal guardians.

**Stability and Supportive Environment:** Courts prioritize the child's best interests when deciding on adoption cases. A good case involves clients demonstrating a stable and supportive environment for the child, including a loving home, financial stability, and a support network.

**Compatibility and Parent-Child Bonding:** A successful adoption involves building a strong bond between the child and the adoptive parents. A good case may involve clients who have developed a positive relationship with the child, showcasing compatibility and a genuine desire to provide a loving and nurturing environment.

To assess if a potential client may have a valid adoption case, ask the following questions.

1. What type of adoption are you considering? Agency adoption, private adoption, domestic adoption, or international adoption?
2. Have you researched and met the eligibility criteria for adoption in your state, including age, marital status, and residency requirements?
3. Have you completed any required background checks or home studies to ensure compliance with legal procedures?
4. Can you demonstrate a stable and supportive environment for the child, including financial stability and a support network?
5. How have you established a bond or relationship with the child you wish to adopt? Can you provide examples of compatibility and your commitment to their well-being?

## Domestic Violence

Domestic violence cases refer to legal matters that involve acts of abuse or violence within intimate relationships, typically between spouses or partners. These cases can encompass various forms of abuse, including physical, emotional, sexual, or financial.

To determine if a potential client has a valid domestic violence case, ask questions such as the following.

1. Have you experienced any form of abuse or violence from your spouse or partner?

2. Are you currently in immediate danger or fear for your safety?
3. Have you reported the incidents of abuse to the police or sought medical attention?
4. Can you provide evidence or documentation, such as photographs, medical records, or witness statements, to support your claims?
5. Are there any previous instances of domestic violence that have occurred?
6. Have you considered obtaining a restraining order or protective order against the abuser?
7. Do you have any concerns about child custody or visitation issues related to domestic violence?
8. Are you aware of any local resources or organizations that support domestic violence victims?

## Personal Injury Law

A personal injury case refers to a legal dispute that arises when an individual suffers harm or injury due to another party's negligence or intentional actions. These cases fall within civil law's jurisdiction and aim to compensate the injured party for their economic and non-economic losses.

Law firms that handle personal injury cases typically work on a contingency basis, meaning they do not charge their clients upfront fees for their legal services. Instead, the attorney's fees are usually based on a percentage of the final settlement or jury award. If the case is unsuccessful and no compensation is obtained, the client does not owe any fees to the law firm.

By operating on a contingency basis, law firms can provide access to legal representation for individuals who may not have the financial means to pay for legal services upfront. It also aligns the law firm's interests with the client, as both parties have a shared goal of securing fair compensation for the injuries sustained.

Understanding how to identify and qualify personal injury cases can help you effectively assess the viability of potential clients and provide valuable guidance to the legal team at your firm. Most personal injury cases have a few things in common. There are various personal injury case types outlined below with unique qualities based on what most law firms look for.

**Duty of Care:** The defendant must have owed a duty of care to the plaintiff (injured party).

**Breach of Duty:** The defendant must have breached their duty through negligent or intentional actions.

**Causation:** The breach of duty must have directly caused the plaintiff's injuries.

**Damages:** The plaintiff must have suffered actual damages, such as medical expenses, lost wages, pain and suffering, or emotional distress.

**Liability:** Assess whether there is evidence to prove the defendant's negligence or wrongdoing.

**Statute of Limitations:** The statute of limitations is a legal time limit within which a person must initiate legal action. It sets the deadline by which the injured party must file a lawsuit or claim for compensation after the incident that caused the injury occurred.

**Insurance Coverage:** Evaluate the availability and adequacy of insurance coverage for potential compensation.

## Motor Vehicle Accidents

Motor vehicle accident cases, also called MVAs, are related to accidents and injuries caused by motor vehicles such as cars, trucks, motorcycles, or bicycles. These cases typically involve personal injury claims and seek compensation for damages incurred due to the negligence or recklessness of another party involved in the accident.

A good case for a lawyer who handles motor vehicle accident cases typically involves the following elements.

**Clear Liability:** A strong case often has clear evidence establishing the liability of another party for the accident, such as police reports, witness statements, video footage, or photographs.

**Negligence:** The injured party must demonstrate that the other party acted negligently and breached their duty of care. Negligence could include actions like speeding, running a red light, drunk driving, or distracted driving.

**Damages:** A successful case should demonstrate the extent of the damages suffered by the injured party, including physical injuries, medical expenses, property damage, lost wages, pain and suffering, and any other relevant losses.

**Statute of Limitations:** The statute of limitations for motor vehicle accidents can vary from state to state. It's important to note the statute of limitations in your state so you can screen cases accordingly.

To determine if a potential client may have a valid motor vehicle accident case, ask the following questions.

1. When and where did the accident occur?
2. Were there any witnesses to the accident? Can you provide their contact information?
3. Have you received medical treatment for your injuries? What injuries did you sustain?
4. Do you have any documentation, such as medical records, photographs, or repair estimates for your vehicle?
5. Was a police report filed? Can you provide a copy, or do you have the police report number?
6. Is your vehicle drivable? Was it towed?
7. Did the other party in the accident admit fault or apologize at the scene?
8. Have you spoken with insurance companies regarding the accident?

## Slip And Fall Incidents

A slip and fall incident case involves legal matters related to injuries sustained by individuals due to hazardous conditions on someone else's property. These cases typically fall under premises liability law, where property owners or occupiers are responsible for maintaining a safe environment for visitors.

These cases typically involve the following elements.

**Hazardous Condition:** A strong case often involves an identifiable hazardous condition on the premises that caused the slip and fall, such as wet or slippery floors, uneven surfaces, inadequate lighting, torn carpets, or other dangerous conditions.

**Property Owner's Negligence:** The injured party must demonstrate that the property owner or occupier was negligent in maintaining the premises, meaning they failed to address the hazardous conditions or did not warn visitors adequately.

**Causation:** The injured party must establish a causal link between the hazardous condition and injuries. It's crucial to prove that the slip and fall incident directly resulted from the dangerous condition, not other unrelated factors.

To determine if a potential client may have a valid slip and fall case, a salesperson can ask the following questions.

1. When and where did the slip and fall incident occur?
2. Can you describe the hazardous condition that caused your fall? Was it a wet surface, uneven flooring, or any other specific hazard?
3. Did you report the incident to the property owner or a responsible person? If yes, what was their response?
4. Did anyone witness the incident? Can you provide their contact information?
5. What injuries did you sustain? Have you sought medical attention for your injuries?
6. Do you have any photographs or documentation of the hazardous condition or your injuries?
7. Were any warning signs or barriers in place to indicate the danger?
8. Have you spoken with insurance companies or anyone involved in the property ownership or management regarding the incident?

## Medical Malpractice

A medical malpractice case involves legal matters related to negligence or misconduct by healthcare professionals that result in harm or injury to a patient. These cases typically arise when a healthcare provider fails to meet the standard of care expected in their profession, leading to detrimental consequences for the patient.

Medical malpractice cases typically involve the following elements.

106

**Doctor-Patient Relationship:** There must be an established doctor-patient relationship, meaning the healthcare professional owes a duty of care to the patient and is responsible for providing medical treatment or advice.

**Breach of Standard of Care:** The injured party must demonstrate that the healthcare provider breached the standard of care expected in their field. This requires showing that the provider acted negligently or deviated from what a reasonably skilled and competent medical professional would have done in similar circumstances.

**Causation:** The injured party must establish a causal link between the healthcare provider's negligence and the resulting harm. The patient must prove that the negligent act or omission directly caused the injuries or worsened the patient's condition.

**Damages:** A successful case should demonstrate the extent of the damages suffered by the patient, including physical injuries, pain and suffering, medical expenses, lost wages, and other relevant losses.

To determine if a potential client may have a valid medical malpractice case, a salesperson can ask the following questions.

1. What medical procedure or treatment did you undergo?
2. Can you describe the specific actions or omissions by the healthcare provider that you believe constituted negligence?
3. What injuries or damages did you suffer? Were there any immediate or long-term consequences of the alleged negligence?
4. Did you seek a second opinion from another medical professional regarding the treatment or procedure?
5. Do any medical records, test results, or other documentation support your claim?
6. Did you discuss your concerns or complaints about the treatment with the healthcare provider or their institution?
7. Have you received any compensation or reimbursement from insurance companies or other parties involved in your medical care?

## Defective Products

A defective product case pertains to legal matters related to injuries or damages caused by a faulty or dangerous product. These cases typically involve claims against manufacturers, distributors, and sellers of products with design flaws, manufacturing defects, or inadequate warnings and instructions.

These cases typically involve the following elements.

**Product Defect:** There must be a clear defect or flaw in the product that renders it unreasonably dangerous or unfit for its intended use. This could include design defects, manufacturing defects, or failures to provide adequate warnings or instructions.

**Causation:** The injured party must establish a causal link between the defect and the resulting injuries or damages. It must be demonstrated that the defect was the primary cause of the harm suffered.

**Foreseeability:** It is essential to show that the defect or danger was reasonably foreseeable by the manufacturer or seller. This means that they should have known about the potential risks associated with the product.

**Damages:** A successful case should demonstrate the extent of the damages suffered by the consumer, including physical injuries, medical expenses, property damage, lost wages, and any relevant losses.

To determine if a potential client may have a valid defective product case, ask the following questions.

1. What product were you using when the incident occurred?
2. Can you describe the specific defect or flaw in the product that caused your injuries or damages?
3. When and where did you purchase the product? Do you still have the receipt or any documentation related to the purchase?
4. What injuries did you sustain? Have you sought medical attention for your injuries?
5. Can you provide photographs or other evidence of the defect or the resulting damages?

6. Did you follow the product's instructions and warnings? Did you use the product in its intended manner?
7. Have there been any recalls or complaints regarding the product? Have you reported the incident to any relevant authorities?
8. Have you contacted the manufacturer, retailer, or insurance companies about the incident?

## Workplace Injuries

A workplace injury case involves legal matters related to injuries or illnesses that occur when a person performs their job duties. These cases fall under workers' compensation laws, where employees are entitled to benefits for work-related injuries or illnesses regardless of fault.

Workplace injury cases involve the following elements.

**Employment Relationship:** The injured party must establish an employment relationship with the employer at the time of the injury, meaning they were an employee and not an independent contractor or volunteer.

**Work-Related Injury or Illness:** The injury or illness must have occurred while the employee performed their job duties or due to their work environment and directly related to their employment.

**Employer's Negligence:** Some cases may involve proving that the employer's negligence contributed to the injury or illness, including situations where the employer failed to provide a safe working environment and proper training, or violated safety regulations.

**Causation:** The injured party must establish a causal link between the workplace conditions and the resulting injury or illness. Employees must prove the work-related factors significantly contributed to the harm suffered.

1. To determine if a potential client may have a valid workplace injury case, ask the following questions.
2. Can you describe the circumstances surrounding the injury or illness at your workplace?

3. When and where did the incident take place? Were you performing your regular job duties at the time?
4. Have you reported the injury or illness to your employer? What was their response?
5. Have you sought medical attention for your injuries or illness? What diagnosis or treatment did you receive?
6. Are there any witnesses to the incident? Can you provide their contact information?
7. Did you document the incident or your symptoms in any way? Do you have any photographs or other evidence?
8. Were there any safety protocols, training, or equipment your employer failed to provide?
9. Have you filed for workers' compensation benefits or spoken with your employer's insurance company regarding the incident?

## Assault or Battery

In personal injury law, the injured person can seek representation for injuries sustained by another person. This situation differs from a criminal law case in which the client defends themselves from criminal charges of assault and battery. A single incident can qualify as a personal injury or criminal case, depending on who is seeking representation.

An assault or battery case involves legal matters related to intentional harm caused to another person. While assault and battery sound similar, they are distinct offenses.

### ASSAULT

The intentional act that creates a reasonable apprehension of harmful or offensive contact with another person. It involves the threat of physical harm without actual physical contact.

### BATTERY

Involves the intentional and unlawful physical contact or harmful touching of another person without their consent.

Assault or battery cases typically involve the following elements.

**Intentional Act:** The injured party must establish that the defendant intentionally committed the act of assault or battery, meaning it was not an accident.

**Apprehension or Harmful Contact:** For an assault case, the injured party must demonstrate that they reasonably feared harmful or offensive contact. There must be evidence of physical contact or harmful touching for a battery case without consent.

**Lack of Consent:** The injured party must prove they did not give consent to the act of assault or battery. Coercion, deception, or incapacity voids consent.

**Damages or Injury:** A successful case demonstrates the extent of the damages or injuries suffered by the victim, including physical injuries, medical expenses, pain and suffering, emotional distress, and any other relevant losses.

To determine if a potential client may have a valid assault or battery case, ask the following questions.

1. Can you describe the incident in detail? What actions did the alleged perpetrator take that made you fear for your safety or caused physical contact without your consent?
2. Did you report the incident to the police or any other authority figure? Do you have a copy of the police report?
3. Are there any witnesses to the incident? Can you provide their contact information?
4. Did you seek medical attention for any injuries sustained? Can you provide documentation of your medical treatment?
5. Have you experienced any emotional distress or other ongoing effects due to the incident?
6. Can any photographs, videos, or other evidence support your claim?
7. Do you have any previous history or relationship with the alleged perpetrator that may be relevant to the case?
8. Have you spoken with any attorneys or legal professionals regarding the incident?

## Dog Bites

When a person is injured or harmed due to a dog attack, they may be entitled to compensation for the damages suffered due to the incident. Dog bites pose a serious health risk, with potential complications such as infections, meningitis, endocarditis, and septic shock leading to death reported in some cases.

When a potential new customer mentions a dog bite case, you should consider identifying factors like the following.

**Liability:** Establishing liability is crucial. The lawyer must determine if the dog's owner or a responsible party can be liable for the bite. This may involve proving negligence, premises liability, or violating local laws or regulations such as leash laws.

**Injury Severity:** The severity of the injuries inflicted by the dog bite plays a significant role. Cases involving severe injuries, such as deep wounds, scarring, disfigurement, or long-term disabilities, generally have a higher chance of success.

**Evidence:** Gathering and preserving evidence is essential for building a strong case. This may include medical records, photographs of injuries, witness statements, veterinary records, and any available video footage or documentation of the incident.

**Provable Damages:** Assessing the potential damage from the dog bite is important. These can include medical expenses, lost wages, pain and suffering, emotional distress, and future medical costs. A lawyer must determine the extent of these damages and gather the necessary documentation.

**Statute of Limitations:** Each state has a specific time limit for the injured party to file a lawsuit. In certain states, the statute of limitations for minors involved in dog bite incidents may differ from that of adults. These states recognize that minors may require additional time to understand the full extent of their injuries or to assert their legal rights.

Here are some questions you can ask to qualify the case.

1. Can you describe how the dog bite happened? What were the circumstances?

2. Was the dog on a leash or otherwise under control?
3. Did the incident occur on public property, such as a park, or private property, such as a residential area?
4. Were there any warning signs or indications of aggressive behavior from the dog or its owner before the bite?
5. Did you seek medical attention after the incident? If so, what were the nature and extent of your injuries?
6. Are there any witnesses to the incident who can provide statements?
7. Have you reported the incident to the appropriate authorities, such as animal control or the police?
8. Are there any photographs or video footage of the incident or your injuries?
9. Have you incurred any medical or other financial losses from the dog bite?
10. How has the incident affected your daily life and overall well-being emotionally and physically?

## Criminal Law

Criminal law cases refer to legal matters with accusations of offenses committed against the state or society. Government authorities typically prosecute these cases and if found guilty, the defendant may face penalties such as fines, probation, or imprisonment.

The following is an overview of the key aspects to consider when evaluating criminal law cases when speaking to someone seeking help from a criminal defense attorney because they are charged with a crime.

**Offense:** Determine what the potential client was charged with. Criminal law covers a wide range of offenses, including but not limited to theft, assault, drug possession, fraud, and homicide.

**Legal Elements:** Assess if the legal elements necessary to prove the offense are present. Each crime has specific elements that must be proven beyond a reasonable doubt for a conviction. You should gather information to determine if these elements will likely be satisfied based on the facts provided.

**Evidence:** Inquire about the evidence available to support the potential client's case. Strong evidence, such as eyewitness testimony, physical evidence, or video footage, can significantly impact the outcome of a criminal trial.

**Client's Role:** Establish the potential client's role in the alleged offense. Were they directly involved in the crime or were they accomplices? Understanding the level of involvement can help assess potential defenses or strategies.

**Legal Defenses:** Identify any potential legal defenses that may apply to the case. Common defenses include self-defense, lack of intent, duress, alibi, or violation of constitutional rights. Assess whether these defenses align with the facts provided by the potential client.

**Prior Record:** Inquire about the potential client's criminal history. A prior record can impact the severity of charges, potential penalties, and the strength of defense strategies.

**Client's Goals:** Understand the potential client's goals and desired outcomes for their case. Some clients may aim for dismissal, acquittal, or reduced charges, while others may focus on minimizing penalties through negotiation or plea bargaining.

**Legal Representation:** Determine if the potential client has already sought legal representation or is actively looking for an attorney to handle their case for the first time.

**Statute of limitations:** Certain serious crimes, such as murder, rape, and some federal offenses, may not have a statute of limitations, meaning the victim can seek prosecution at any time. However, there are statutes of limitations with some types of cases in certain states. For example, a state may have a shorter statute of limitations for misdemeanors than felonies. Additionally, federal crimes have their limitations outlined by federal law.

## DUI/DWI defense

DUI/DWI defense cases occur when individuals operate a vehicle while allegedly impaired by alcohol, drugs, or a combination of both. If the potential new customer shares anything that may indicate potential legal issues with the traffic stop, sobriety testing, chemical test results, Miranda rights violation, or other factors that could impact the case, it suggests that the case may be worth pursuing with the assistance of a lawyer specializing in DUI/DWI defense.

DUI/DWI defense cases typically involve the following elements.

**Traffic Stop and Arrest:** The lawyer must assess whether the police conducted the traffic stop and subsequent arrest lawfully, including determining if the police had reasonable suspicion or probable cause to stop the vehicle and make the arrest.

**Sobriety Testing:** It is important to examine the procedures used for sobriety testing, such as field sobriety or breathalyzer tests. Any issues with the administration or accuracy of these tests can be crucial in building a strong defense.

**Chemical Test Results:** If a chemical test (such as a blood, breath, or urine test) is conducted, the lawyer will evaluate the accuracy and reliability of the test results. Factors include the calibration of the testing equipment and the qualifications of the testing personnel.

**Miranda Rights:** The lawyer will determine if the police read the defendant's Miranda rights properly and if the police obtained any statements made during the arrest in violation of those rights.

**Documentation and Evidence:** Gathering all relevant documents and evidence—including police reports, witness statements, surveillance footage, audio recordings, or any other information that can support the defense—is crucial.

To determine if a potential client may have a valid DUI/DWI defense case, ask the following questions.

1. Can you describe the circumstances leading up to your arrest for DUI/DWI? What prompted the traffic stop?
2. When and where were you stopped?
3. Were any field sobriety tests conducted? If so, did you feel the police administered them fairly and accurately?

4. Were you asked to perform a breathalyzer or other chemical test for determining blood alcohol concentration (BAC)? Do you have any concerns about the accuracy or reliability of the test?
5. Were your Miranda rights read to you during the arrest? Were any statements you made used against you?
6. Have you received any arrest documentation, such as police reports or citations?
7. Can witnesses support your version of events or testify to your sobriety during the incident?
8. Have you had any prior DUI/DWI convictions or encounters with law enforcement that may impact your case?
9. As far as you know, was your ability to drive impaired by any alcohol, drugs, or prescribed medications?
10. Do you have any health conditions that may interfere with your ability to drive?

## Drug Offenses

If a potential client mentions drug charges, it is important to note that federal and state laws that outline the specific drugs involved and the corresponding penalties govern these cases. As you gather details about the case from the potential new client, look for signs that indicate potential legal issues that weaken the case against them, including issues with the search and seizure, possession or distribution claims, violation of constitutional rights, or other factors that could impact the case.

Look for elements such as the following.

**Search and Seizure:** The lawyer must assess whether the search and seizure of drugs or related evidence were conducted lawfully, including determining if law enforcement had a valid search warrant or if the search fell within a recognized exception to the warrant requirement.

**Possession or Distribution:** The lawyer will need to evaluate whether there is sufficient evidence to establish the defendant's possession or involvement in the distribution of controlled substances. This may include considering the proximity of drugs, witness statements, surveillance footage, or any other evidence linking the defendant to the offense.

**Chain of Custody:** If the police seized drugs or other physical evidence, the lawyer would examine the chain of custody to ensure that the evidence was properly handled, stored, and preserved. Any gaps or inconsistencies in the chain of custody can be used to challenge the admissibility of the evidence.

**Constitutional Rights:** The lawyer will investigate whether the police violated the defendant's constitutional rights during the arrest, search, or seizure. This investigation includes examining issues such as unlawful detention, coerced confessions, or violations of Miranda rights.

**Lab Analysis:** If the police conducted drug testing, the lawyer will assess the accuracy and reliability of the laboratory analysis by scrutinizing the testing personnel's qualifications, equipment calibration, and adherence to proper procedures.

To determine if a potential client may have a valid drug offense case, ask the following questions.

1. Can you provide details about the circumstances surrounding your arrest for drug offenses? How did law enforcement initially contact you?
2. Did law enforcement have a search warrant when they discovered the drugs or was the search conducted without one? If it was a warrantless search, do you believe there were any legal issues with the search?
3. What type of drugs were involved in the case? Were they found in your possession, or are you accused of being involved in distribution or trafficking?
4. Are you concerned about the evidence or how the police handled it? Were the drugs properly identified and preserved from the seizure to the lab analysis?
5. Did law enforcement read you your Miranda rights during the arrest? Did you make any statements against you without proper advisement of your rights?

6. Have you been charged with drug offenses in the past? Have you completed any rehabilitation programs or taken steps to address substance abuse issues?

## Assault and Battery

As discussed above, assault and battery are separate but related offenses in criminal law. Assault involves the intentional act causing someone to fear imminent physical harm, even if no contact occurs. Battery involves the intentional and unlawful use of force or violence against another person. Both can result in criminal charges and consequences, and the severity of penalties depends on the circumstances and local laws.

The following are some key factors for a strong defense in assault and battery cases to consider:

**Evidence Weakness:** Lack of substantial evidence or inconsistencies in the evidence can weaken the prosecution's case. This could include witness statements, video footage, or physical evidence.

**Self-defense:** It could be a strong defense strategy if the defendant acted in self-defense or in defense of others. Clear evidence supporting this claim is crucial.

**Mistaken Identity:** If there's doubt regarding the assailant's identity or confusion about the events, it can weaken the case against the defendant.

**Consent or Provocation:** In some cases, consent or mutual combat can be a defense if both parties willingly agree to engage in the altercation. If the defendant can prove that they were provoked or incited to commit the assault and battery, it might mitigate the charges.

**Witness Credibility:** The credibility of witnesses plays a significant role. If the defense can challenge the reliability or credibility of prosecution witnesses, it might weaken their case.

**Expert Testimony:** Expert witnesses, such as psychologists or medical professionals, can sometimes provide valuable testimony that supports the defense's case.

**Alibi:** If the defendant can provide a strong alibi, proving they were not at the location at the time of the incident, it can be a powerful defense.

**Police Conduct:** Any misconduct by law enforcement officers during the arrest or investigation could be grounds for dismissal or weakening of the case.

**Prior Criminal Record:** The defendant's criminal record (or lack thereof) can influence sentencing or plea bargain negotiations.

When evaluating whether a potential client has an assault and battery case under criminal law, there are several key questions you might consider asking.

1. What exactly happened? Can you describe the events leading up to and during the incident?
2. Did you intentionally cause harm or threaten someone? Were you aware of your actions at the time?
3. Was there any physical contact involved? If so, what type and to what extent?
4. Did the other person express fear or feel threatened by your actions? Was there any verbal threat or indication of imminent harm?
5. Were you defending yourself or someone else? Was there any provocation or escalation from the other party?
6. Are there any witnesses or evidence supporting your version of events? This could include videos, photos, or testimonies from bystanders.
7. Have any previous altercations or legal issues involving the same parties?
8. Were there any injuries sustained by either party? How severe were they?
9. Have law enforcement questioned or arrested you regarding this incident?

## White-collar Crimes

A white-collar crime case involves legal matters related to non-violent offenses typically committed by business professionals or individuals in positions of power. These crimes are often financially motivated and involve deceit, fraud, or illegal actions in the corporate or financial realm.

White-collar crimes typically involve the following elements.

**Complexity of the Offense:** White-collar crimes are often intricate and involve complex financial transactions, corporate structures, or sophisticated schemes. A strong case may involve multiple layers of evidence requiring meticulous analysis and understanding of financial records, contracts, or digital evidence.

**Intent and Knowledge:** The lawyer will assess whether there is evidence to establish the defendant's intent and knowledge of their alleged illegal actions. Proving intent is crucial in white-collar crime cases, as it demonstrates a deliberate and conscious effort to engage in fraudulent or deceptive practices.

**Financial Impact:** The lawyer will evaluate the extent of the financial harm caused by the alleged white-collar crime, including determining the amount of money involved, the number of victims affected, or the impact on businesses or the economy.

**Compliance and Regulatory Issues:** White-collar crime cases often intersect with complex regulatory frameworks. The lawyer must deeply understand relevant laws and regulations specific to the industry. They will assess compliance issues or violations that could impact the case outcome.

**Evidence Collection:** White-collar crime cases rely on documentary evidence, such as financial records, contracts, emails, or other electronic communications. The lawyer must ensure proper collection, preservation, and analysis of this evidence to build a strong defense or prosecution strategy.

To determine if a potential client may have a valid white-collar crime case, ask the following questions.

1. Can you describe the nature of the alleged white-collar crime? What specific actions or behaviors are you accused of engaging in?
2. What evidence, if any, do you have to support your defense? Are there any documents or records that can help establish your innocence or challenge the accusations?

3. Were any compliance or regulatory issues involved in the alleged offense? Were you aware of any violations, or did you take steps to ensure adherence to relevant laws and regulations?
4. What was the financial impact of the alleged crime? Can you estimate the monetary value and number of individuals or entities affected?
5. Have you been contacted by any regulatory agencies or law enforcement regarding the alleged white-collar crime? If so, what actions have been taken so far?
6. Do you have legal representation currently, or are you actively seeking a lawyer to handle your case?

## Real Estate Law

A real estate case involves legal matters related to property transactions, disputes, and regulations. These cases can encompass various aspects of real estate, such as buying, selling, leasing, financing, or developing properties. Qualifying leads for real estate law cases involves asking relevant questions to determine if a potential client may have a valid case.

The following are some real estate case types involving disputes.

### Property Purchase/Sale Disputes

You can ask if the potential new client is involved in a dispute regarding a real estate purchase or sale dispute, including contract issues, nondisclosure of defects, breach of contract, title disputes, or property misrepresentations.

Following are sample questions you can use to qualify this case type.

1. Were you involved in a recent real estate transaction?
2. What specific issues or concerns do you have with the transaction?
3. Have you experienced problems with the property's condition or title after the purchase/sale?

### Landlord-tenant Disputes

Determine if the individual seeking legal help faces conflicts or issues as a landlord or a tenant, such as eviction, lease violations, security deposit disputes, or property maintenance problems.

Following are questions you can use to evaluate if a potential new customer has a landlord-tenant dispute case.

1. Are you currently renting a property, or do you own rental properties?
2. What specific problems are you facing with your tenant/landlord?
3. Have there been any breaches of the lease agreement or failure to address maintenance issues?

**Zoning and Land Use Issues:** Explore if the potential client requires legal assistance with zoning regulations, land use restrictions, or development projects. This may involve obtaining permits, addressing code violations, or appealing zoning decisions.

Explore whether the potential new customer has a zoning and land use issue with the following questions.

1. Are you planning to develop or modify a property?
2. Have you encountered any zoning or land use permit challenges?
3. Are there any code violations or disputes with local authorities?

**Real Estate Financing and Foreclosure:** Determine if the individual seeks help with mortgage-related matters, refinancing, or foreclosure defense. These cases may involve modifications, predatory lending, or wrongful foreclosure actions.

Ask the following questions to determine if this is your potential new customer's case.

1. Are you currently facing foreclosure or struggling with mortgage payments?
2. Have you experienced any issues with your lender or mortgage servicer?
3. Are you interested in exploring options for loan modification or refinancing?

**Construction and Contract Disputes:** Inquire if the potential client requires assistance with construction defects, contractor disputes, or breach of contract issues related to real estate projects.

Ask the following questions.:

1. Were you involved in a construction project that encountered problems or defects?
2. Are there any disputes with contractors, subcontractors, or suppliers?
3. Has there been any breach of contract or failure to meet agreed-upon terms?

## Residential Property Disputes

A residential property dispute case involves legal issues and conflicts related to residential properties, such as homes, apartments, or condominiums. These cases can arise from various disputes between landlords and tenants, homeowners and neighbors, or co-owners of a property. The goal is to resolve conflicts and establish legal rights and responsibilities concerning residential properties.

Residential property disputes typically involve the following elements.

**Lease Agreement Violations:** The lawyer will assess whether there are any breaches of the lease agreement by either the landlord or the tenant, which can include issues such as nonpayment of rent, failure to address maintenance requests, improper eviction procedures, or unauthorized changes to the premises.

**Property Damage Claims:** The lawyer will evaluate if claims are related to property damage caused by either party, which involves assessing the extent of the damage, determining liability, and seeking appropriate compensation for repairs or losses.

**Landlord-tenant Disputes:** The lawyer will examine conflicts between landlords and tenants, such as eviction disputes, wrongful withholding of security deposits, illegal entry by the landlord, or harassment by either party. Resolving these conflicts requires a thorough understanding of landlord-tenant laws and regulations.

**Neighbor Disputes:** The lawyer will address conflicts between neighbors, including boundary disputes, noise complaints, property encroachments, or nuisance issues. Resolving these disputes may involve interpreting property boundaries, examining local ordinances, or negotiating agreements between the parties involved.

To determine if a potential client may have a valid residential property dispute case, ask the following questions.

1. Are you currently renting a residential property, or do you own one?
2. What issues or conflicts are you facing with your landlord, tenant, or neighbor?
3. Has there been any breach of the lease agreement, such as non-payment of rent or failure to address maintenance requests?
4. Are there any claims related to property damage caused by the other party? Can you provide details about the extent of the damage and any expenses incurred?
5. Have you faced eviction proceedings or harassment from your landlord, tenant, or neighbor?
6. Is there a dispute regarding property boundaries, noise complaints, or other nuisance issues with your neighbor?

## Commercial Property Transactions

A commercial property transactions case involves legal matters related to buying, selling, leasing, or developing commercial properties. These cases focus on commercial real estate, which includes properties used for business purposes such as offices, retail spaces, industrial facilities, or multi-unit residential complexes. The goal is to navigate complex transactions, ensure compliance with relevant laws and regulations, and protect the rights and interests of the parties involved.

Commercial property transactions typically involve the following elements.

**Purchase and Sale Agreements:** The lawyer will assess whether there are disputes or issues arising from the purchase or sale of commercial properties, which can include matters related to contract breaches, misrepresentations, title defects, financing problems, or failure to disclose material information.

**Lease Agreements and Negotiations:** The lawyer will evaluate conflicts or disputes related to commercial lease agreements, which can involve issues like lease enforcement, rent disputes, tenant improvements, lease terminations, or disagreements over lease terms and conditions.

**Zoning and Land Use Regulations:** The lawyer will address challenges associated with zoning and land use regulations that may impact commercial property transactions, including obtaining necessary permits, complying with zoning restrictions, addressing code violations, or navigating environmental compliance.

**Development Projects:** The lawyer will handle legal matters related to the development of commercial properties, which can involve contract negotiations, construction disputes, land acquisition, regulatory compliance, financing arrangements, or issues with architects, contractors, or subcontractors.

To determine if a potential client may have a valid commercial property transactions case, ask the following questions.

1. Are you involved in purchasing or selling a commercial property?
2. What specific issues or conflicts have arisen during the transaction?
3. Has there been any breach of the purchase and sale agreement or misrepresentation by the other party?
4. Are there any concerns related to the title or financing of the commercial property?
5. Are you seeking assistance with negotiating or reviewing commercial lease agreements?
6. Are there any disputes or disagreements regarding lease enforcement, rent payments, or lease termination?
7. Are you planning a commercial development project? What specific challenges or legal matters are you facing?
8. Are there any zoning or land use restrictions that may impact your commercial property transaction or development project?

## Residential Property Transactions

These cases include legal matters related to buying or leasing a property. A potential new client may contact a law firm for assistance before or after a transaction, primarily for help with an agreement creation or review.

Several factors can significantly impact a residential property case. The following are some crucial elements:

**Contractual Obligations:** The terms and conditions outlined in the purchase agreement are legally binding for both the buyer and seller. Any breach of contract can lead to legal disputes.

**Property Disclosures:** Laws often require sellers to disclose known defects or issues with the property. Failure to disclose material defects can result in legal action by the buyer.

**Title Issues:** Title searches are crucial to ensure clear ownership. Disputes over property boundaries, liens, encroachments, or easements can lead to legal conflicts.

**Financing and Mortgage Issues:** Disputes can arise regarding loan conditions, mortgage fraud, or issues related to the lender's failure to fund the purchase.

**Misrepresentation or Fraud:** Cases may involve allegations of misrepresentation or fraud by either party, such as misstating property conditions or withholding information.

**Home Inspection Problems:** Disputes may arise if the property inspection reveals issues not previously disclosed or addressed in negotiations.

**Failure to Close:** Circumstances leading to the failure to close the transaction, whether due to one party's inability to meet conditions or any other factor, can result in legal actions for damages or specific performance.

**Contingencies and Timelines**: Violating agreed-upon contingencies or timelines specified in the contract can lead to disputes and potential legal actions.

**Rescission or Termination:** Instances where one party seeks to rescind or terminate the contract due to legal reasons or breaches by the other party fall into this category.

To determine if a potential client may have a valid residential property transactions case, ask the following questions.

1. What type of property transaction occurred or are you planning to engage in?

2. Are there specific concerns about the transaction?
3. Were there written agreements, and were they followed?
4. Any undisclosed property issues or false representations?
5. Any disputes over property ownership, liens, or title?
6. Were there title searches and if so, were issues found?
7. Were there problems with financing, lender actions, or failed closing?
8. Any attempts to terminate the transaction and if so, for what reasons?
9. Did both parties comply with laws and disclosures?
10. Are there any concerns about legal compliance during the transaction?
11. Were agents involved, and were there conduct issues?

## Landlord-tenant Issues

A landlord-tenant issues case involves legal matters and disputes between landlords and tenants. These cases encompass various conflicts arising from the landlord-tenant relationship, such as lease violations, eviction proceedings, security deposit disputes, maintenance and repair issues, and breaches of rental agreements.

Landlord-tenant issues typically involve the following elements.

**Lease Agreement Violations:** The lawyer will assess any lease agreement breaches by either the landlord or the tenant, including nonpayment of rent, failure to maintain the property, unauthorized alterations, or violations of specific lease terms.

**Eviction Proceedings:** The lawyer will handle cases related to eviction, ensuring that the landlord follows proper procedures and legal requirements, including termination notices, unlawful detainer actions, wrongful evictions, or defenses against eviction.

**Security Deposit Disputes:** The lawyer will address conflicts over security deposits, including improper withholding, deductions, or failure to return the deposit within the required timeframe. Resolving these disputes may involve reviewing lease agreements, documenting damages, and asserting the tenant's rights.

**Maintenance and Repair Issues:** The lawyer will evaluate cases where landlords fail to address necessary repairs or maintain the habitability of the rental property, including plumbing problems, heating or cooling failures, pest infestations, or hazardous conditions.

To determine if a potential client may have a valid landlord-tenant issues case, ask the following questions.

1. Are you currently renting a property, or do you own rental properties?
2. What issues or conflicts are you facing with your landlord or tenant?
3. Has there been any breach of the lease agreement, such as non-payment of rent or failure to address maintenance requests?
4. Are you currently involved in eviction proceedings, or have you received termination notices from your landlord?
5. Are there any disputes regarding the security deposit, including improper withholding or deductions?
6. Have you experienced problems related to maintenance and repairs in your rental property?
7. Can you provide any documentation or evidence to support your claims?

## Zoning and Land Use

A zoning and land use case involves legal matters related to land development, land regulations, and zoning ordinances. These cases focus on disputes and conflicts arising from land use, development, or modification, including rezoning, variances, permits, restrictions, or violations of land use regulations.

Zoning and land use cases typically involve the following elements.

**Zoning Ordinance Compliance:** The lawyer will assess whether there are violations or disputes regarding zoning regulations, which include conflicts related to land use restrictions, setbacks, building heights, density requirements, parking regulations, or permitted uses.

**Land Development Approvals:** The lawyer will handle cases involving the approval process for land development projects, which can include challenges associated with obtaining zoning approvals, special permits, variances, or conditional use permits from local planning or zoning boards.

**Environmental Concerns:** The lawyer will address legal issues related to environmental regulations and impacts on land use, which include matters such as wetland protection, environmental impact assessments, water resource management, or compliance with environmental standards.

**Eminent Domain and Condemnation:** The lawyer may handle eminent domain cases where the government acquires private property for public use, which includes evaluating compensation offers, negotiating fair market value, or challenging the legality of the condemnation process.

To determine if a potential client may have a valid zoning and land use case, ask the following questions.

1. Are you planning any land development projects or modifications to your property?
2. Have you encountered any challenges or disputes regarding zoning regulations or land use restrictions?
3. Are you seeking approvals or permits from local planning or zoning boards for your development project?
4. Have you received any notices or citations indicating violations of zoning ordinances or land use regulations?
5. Are environmental concerns or regulations affecting your property or development plans?
6. Have you been approached by the government or a public agency for the potential acquisition of your property under eminent domain?

## Intellectual Property Law

An intellectual property law case involves legal matters related to protecting and enforcing intellectual property rights. Intellectual property refers to intangible creations of the mind, such as inventions, designs, trademarks, copyrights, and trade secrets. These cases focus on securing rights to intellectual property and disputes arising from unauthorized use, infringement, or misappropriation of intellectual property.

Intellectual property law cases can include various case types such as the following.

## Trademark Registration

Trademark registration cases involve legal matters related to the registration and protection of trademarks. A trademark is a distinctive sign, symbol, word, or phrase that identifies and distinguishes the source of goods or services. The potential new customer will need a lawyer to handle cases related to the application process for trademark registration, which includes ensuring that the proposed trademark is distinctive, conducting thorough searches to identify potential conflicts with existing trademarks, and preparing and submitting the application to the United States Patent and Trademark Office (USPTO). You should gather information about the nature of the mark, its uniqueness, and its intended use.

To determine if a potential client may have a valid trademark registration case, ask the following questions.

1. Have you created a unique symbol, logo, word, or phrase you use to identify your goods or services?
2. How has the mark been used? What are your intentions for its future use?
3. What goods or services does the mark represent?
4. Who will own the trademark?
5. What are your plans to involve the mark?
6. Have you registered your trademark with the USPTO?
7. Are you aware of any instances where others use a similar or identical trademark without permission?
8. Has this unauthorized use confused consumers or affected your brand's reputation?
9. Has the USPTO rejected your trademark registration application and if so, on what grounds?
10. Have you received any notices or communications regarding potential trademark infringements?

## Trademark Maintenance and Protection

A lawyer can assist in monitoring and protecting registered trademarks against unauthorized use or infringement, which can involve sending cease and desist letters, initiating opposition or cancellation proceedings, or taking legal action to enforce trademark rights.

To determine if a potential client may have a valid trademark maintenance and protection case, ask the following questions.

1. Do you have a registered trademark with the USPTO?
2. Are you aware of any instances where others use a similar or identical trademark?
3. How consistently and prominently has the trademark been used in commerce?
4. Have the necessary renewal filings been consistently made, and is the trademark compliant with maintenance requirements?
5. Have there been changes associated with the trademark since its registration?
6. Is there a need for international protection or expansion of the trademark's geographic scope?

## Trademark Infringement

Potential new customers may have a valid case if they believe their registered trademark has been used without authorization, leading to confusion or dilution of their brand identity. It helps to assess if there are instances where another party uses a similar or identical trademark without authorization, causing confusion among consumers or diluting the brand identity, including unauthorized use in advertising, packaging, or selling competing goods or services.

Trademark infringement typically involves the following elements.

**Valid Trademark:** The lawyer will assess if the client has a registered trademark with the USPTO or has developed common law rights through extensive use and recognition in commerce. A valid trademark provides the basis for pursuing legal action against infringers.

**Likelihood of Confusion:** The lawyer will evaluate whether the unauthorized use of the mark is likely to confuse consumers. The court will consider factors such as the similarity of the marks, the relatedness of the goods or services, and the strength of the mark when determining the potential for confusion.

**Actual Use in Commerce:** The lawyer will investigate whether the infringing party is using the mark in commerce, which typically involves the sale or advertising of goods or services. This element is crucial in proving trademark infringement and seeking appropriate remedies.

**Damages or Likelihood of Harm:** The lawyer may assess the impact of the infringement on the client's business, such as lost sales, damage to reputation, or dilution of the trademark's distinctiveness. Demonstrating actual or potential harm strengthens the case for seeking damages or injunctive relief.

To determine if a potential client may have a valid trademark infringement case, ask the following questions.

1. Do you have a registered trademark with the USPTO?
2. Are you aware of any instances where others use a similar or identical trademark?
3. How similar is the trademark of the infringing party offering the goods or services to yours?
4. Has the unauthorized use of the mark caused any confusion among consumers?
5. Are you currently using the mark in commerce, and can you provide evidence of this use?
6. Have you experienced any tangible damages, loss of sales, or harm to your brand's reputation due to the infringement?

## Copyright Infringement

Potential new customers may have a valid case if they believe their original creative works such as books, music, films, or software have been copied, distributed, or performed without permission.

Qualifying questions can include the following.

1. Have you created an original work protected by copyright?

2. Are you aware of any instances where others have used your work without permission?
3. Has this unauthorized use impacted your ability to profit from or control your work?

## Patent Infringement

Potential new customers may have a valid case if they believe their patented invention or technology has been used, manufactured, or sold by others without authorization.

Qualifying questions can include the following.

1. Do you hold a granted patent for your invention or technology?
2. Are you aware of any instances where others use or sell a similar invention?
3. Has this unauthorized use affected your ability to monetize your invention or protect your market share?

## Trade Secret Misappropriation

Leads may have a valid case if they believe their confidential business information, such as formulas, processes, or customer lists, has been unlawfully disclosed or used by others.

Qualifying questions can include the following.

1. Do you have valuable and confidential business information that provides a competitive advantage?
2. Are you aware of any instances where this information has been shared or used without permission?
3. Has this unauthorized disclosure or use harmed your business or market position?

## Patent Disputes

A patent dispute case involves legal matters related to protecting and enforcing patent rights. A patent is a form of intellectual property that grants exclusive rights to inventors for their inventions, preventing others from making, using, or selling the patented invention without permission.

Patent dispute cases typically arise when there are conflicts over a patent's validity, ownership, or infringement and involve the following elements.

**Valid and Enforceable Patent:** The lawyer will assess if the client's invention is eligible for patent protection and if the USPTO has granted a valid patent. The lawyer will also consider if the patent is still in force and hasn't expired.

**Patent Infringement:** The lawyer will evaluate whether another party is using, manufacturing, selling, or importing a product or process that falls within the scope of the client's patented invention without authorization, which requires demonstrating that the infringing party's product or process includes all the essential elements of the patented invention.

**Ownership and Assignment:** The lawyer may handle cases where there are disputes regarding the ownership or assignment of a patent, which can include situations where multiple parties claim ownership or contractual agreements related to the patent rights.

**Damages or Injunctive Relief:** The lawyer will assess the damages suffered by the patent holder due to the infringement and determine the appropriate remedies, which may include monetary compensation or seeking an injunction to stop the infringing activities.

To determine if a potential client may have a valid patent dispute case, ask the following questions.

1. Have you been granted a patent by the USPTO for your invention?
2. Are you aware of any parties using, manufacturing, or selling a product or process similar to your patented invention without your permission?
3. Does the infringing product or process include all the essential elements of your patented invention?
4. Can you provide evidence of the infringing activities, such as documentation, samples, or photographs?
5. Have you suffered any financial damages or loss of market share due to the infringement?
6. Are there any disputes or issues regarding the ownership or assignment of the patent?

# Copyright Registration

A copyright registration case involves legal matters related to the registration and protection of creative works, such as literary, artistic, musical, or dramatic. Copyright registration is a process through which authors or creators can secure legal rights and protections for their original works. Copyright registration cases often revolve around disputes and conflicts regarding ownership, infringement, or unauthorized use of copyrighted materials.

Copyright registration typically involves the following elements.

**Original and Creative Work:** The lawyer will assess if the client's work meets the criteria for copyright protection, which requires the work to be original and fixed in a tangible medium of expression, which includes written content, visual art, music, films, software, or other creative forms.

**Copyright Registration:** The lawyer will handle cases related to the registration process for copyright protection, which involves preparing and submitting the necessary application to the United States Copyright Office and ensuring compliance with the registration requirements.

**Copyright Infringement:** The lawyer will evaluate whether another party has copied, distributed, displayed, performed, or adapted the copyrighted work without authorization. Copyright infringement occurs when someone violates the copyright owner's exclusive rights, such as making unauthorized reproductions or derivative works.

**Ownership and Licensing:** The lawyer may assist in cases where there are disputes over ownership or licensing rights of copyrighted works, which can include situations where multiple parties claim ownership or where others have violated licensing agreements.

To determine if a potential client may have a valid copyright registration case, ask the following questions.

1. Have you created an original and creative work, such as a book, song, artwork, or software?

2. Have you registered your copyright with the United States Copyright Office?
3. Are you aware of any instances where others have used your copyrighted work without permission?
4. How has the unauthorized use of your work impacted your rights or commercial interests?
5. Can you provide evidence of the infringement, such as copies, recordings, or documentation?
6. Are there any disputes or issues regarding the ownership or licensing of the copyrighted work?

## Copyright Violations

A copyright violation case involves legal matters related to the unauthorized use, reproduction, distribution, or display of copyrighted materials without the copyright owner's permission. Copyright violations occur when someone infringes upon the exclusive rights granted to the creator or owner of a protected work. These cases often revolve around disputes regarding unauthorized copying, plagiarism, or infringement of intellectual property rights. Copyright violation typically involves the following elements:

**Valid Copyright:** The lawyer will assess if the client's work–such as literary works, music, films, artwork, software, or other creative forms–is eligible for copyright protection. A valid copyright provides the basis for pursuing legal action against infringers.

**Proof of Infringement:** The lawyer will evaluate whether another party has used, copied, or distributed the copyrighted work without authorization, which requires demonstrating that the infringing party's work is substantially similar or identical to the original.

**Ownership and Registration:** The lawyer may handle cases where there are disputes over ownership or registration of the copyright. It is important to establish that the client is the rightful owner of the copyrighted material and that the creator properly registered the work with the United States Copyright Office.

**Damages or Losses**: The lawyer will assess the impact of the copyright violation on the client's rights or commercial interests, which can include calculating financial damages, loss of licensing opportunities, harm to reputation, or other negative consequences resulting from the infringement.

To determine if a potential client may have a valid copyright violation case, ask the following questions.

1. Have you created an original work eligible for copyright protection?
2. Are you aware of any instances where someone has used, copied, or distributed your copyrighted work without permission?
3. Can you provide evidence or examples showing the similarity between your copyrighted work and the infringing work?
4. Have you registered your copyright with the United States Copyright Office?
5. How has the unauthorized use of your work affected your rights or commercial interests?
6. Are there any disputes or issues regarding the ownership or registration of the copyrighted work?

## Trade Secret Protection

A trade secret protection case involves legal matters related to safeguarding and enforcing valuable confidential information that provides a competitive advantage to a business. Trade secrets can include formulas, processes, techniques, customer lists, or any other nonpublic information that is kept confidential and gives a business a competitive edge. Trade secret protection cases typically revolve around disputes regarding misappropriation, unauthorized disclosure, or theft of confidential information and involve the following elements.

**Confidential Information:** The lawyer will assess if the client's information meets the criteria for a trade secret, such as being valuable, not generally known, and subject to reasonable efforts to maintain secrecy, which includes proprietary formulas, strategies, customer lists, or confidential business information.

**Misappropriation:** The lawyer will evaluate whether another party has acquired, used, or disclosed the trade secret without authorization, which requires demonstrating that the defendant had access to the trade secret and that they improperly acquired, disclosed, or used it.

**Reasonable Efforts to Maintain Secrecy:** The lawyer will examine whether the client took reasonable measures to protect the confidentiality of the trade secret., which can include implementing confidentiality agreements, restricted access, password protection, nondisclosure policies, or other security measures.

**Damages or Injunctive Relief:** The lawyer will assess the economic harm suffered by the trade secret owner due to the misappropriation and determine the appropriate remedies, which may involve seeking monetary compensation or obtaining an injunction to prevent further use or disclosure of the trade secret.

To determine if a potential client may have a valid trade secret protection case, ask the following questions.

1. Do you possess valuable confidential information that provides a competitive advantage to your business?
2. Have you taken reasonable measures to maintain the secrecy of this information, such as implementing confidentiality agreements or access controls?
3. Are you aware of any instances where someone has acquired, used, or disclosed your trade secret without authorization?
4. Can you provide evidence or examples showing that the defendant had access to the trade secret and improperly used or disclosed it?
5. How has the misappropriation of your trade secret affected your competitive position or caused economic harm to your business?
6. Are there any contractual agreements or confidentiality policies in place that govern the protection of your trade secrets?

## Intellectual Property

Intellectual property (IP) refers to creations of the mind, such as inventions, designs, trademarks, copyrights, and trade secrets. An intellectual property case typically arises when a dispute or infringement is related to these protected assets. It can also include cases where someone accuses a company or individual of using their intellectual property without permission.

To determine if a case is viable, you must first assess the strength of the IP protection in question, if there is one, which can involve reviewing registration certificates, licenses, or any other documentation that establishes intellectual property ownership. A strong and valid protection will greatly increase the chances of success in court.

Look for the following key terms when qualifying a prospect.

**Infringement:** A strong IP case involves clear evidence of someone using, reproducing, or exploiting another party's protected intellectual property without permission, thereby infringing upon their rights.

**Valid Intellectual Property Rights:** Cases where the client can demonstrate legally recognized intellectual property rights, such as patents, trademarks, copyrights, or trade secrets, provide a solid foundation for legal action.

**Registration or Documentation:** Having registered intellectual property rights with the appropriate government authorities or having proper documentation such as copyrights or trademark registrations, strengthens the case by providing formal recognition and evidence of ownership.

**Damages or Harm:** Cases where the infringement has resulted in quantifiable damages or harm to the IP owner, such as lost profits or a negative impact on their brand or reputation, enhance the chances of a successful case.

**Prior Warning or Cease-and-Desist:** If the IP owner has previously warned the alleged infringer or sent a cease-and-desist letter, it can bolster the case by demonstrating an attempt to resolve the matter amicably before resorting to legal action.

To determine if a potential client may have a valid intellectual property case, the following are some questions that a salesperson can ask.

1. Do you have any intellectual property assets, such as inventions, designs, trademarks, copyrights, or trade secrets?
2. Have you identified instances of someone using, reproducing, or exploiting your intellectual property without permission?
3. Do you have valid and recognized intellectual property rights, such as patents, trademarks, copyrights, or trade secrets?
4. Have you registered your intellectual property rights with the appropriate government authorities?
5. Do you need assistance registering or protecting intellectual property assets?
6. Have you incurred any quantifiable damages or harm due to the infringement?
7. Have you previously warned the alleged infringer or sent a cease-and-desist letter?

## Immigration Law

An immigration law case involves legal matters related to individuals seeking entry, residency, or citizenship in the United States. Immigration law governs the complex rules, regulations, and processes determining immigrants' eligibility, rights, and obligations. These cases revolve around visa applications, family-based petitions, employment authorizations, deportation defense, asylum claims, or naturalization.

For an immigration case, consider the following factors.

**Immigration Status:** Determine the current immigration status of the potential client. Are they nonimmigrants on a temporary visa, lawful permanent residents (green-card holders), or undocumented immigrants? These questions will help assess the type of case they may need assistance with.

**Specific Immigration Need:** Identify the specific immigration need or concern the client has. Are they looking to apply for a family-based visa, seek asylum, obtain a work permit, defend against deportation, or pursue naturalization? Understanding their objective will help determine if the law firm can provide the necessary legal services.

**Legal Issues or Challenges:** Assess if there are any legal issues or challenges involved in the case. For example, has the client faced previous immigration violations, criminal convictions, or removal proceedings? Understanding these factors will help gauge the case's complexity and whether specialized expertise is required.

**Timeline and Urgency:** Determine if the client has any urgent needs or impending deadlines, such as an upcoming court appearance or visa expiration. This information will help prioritize and manage the case effectively.

**Financial Considerations:** Discuss the client's ability to pay for legal services. Immigration cases can be costly, so understanding the client's financial situation will help determine if they are eligible for payment plans, pro bono services, or other forms of assistance.

**Documentation and Eligibility:** Inquire about the client's access to necessary documentation and evidence to support their case, including passports, birth certificates, marriage certificates, employment records, or any other relevant paperwork. Assessing their eligibility based on the available information is crucial.

## Visa Applications and Appeals

A visa application and appeals case involves legal matters related to individuals applying for visas or appealing for visa denials. A visa is an official document issued by a country that permits a foreign national to enter, stay, or work in that country for a specific period. Visa applications and appeals cases typically involve visa eligibility, documentation, compliance with immigration laws, and challenging visa denials or revocations.

Note that in the case of immigration, it's important to prequalify as much as possible but ultimately, let an attorney evaluate each person's circumstances to see if they qualify for immigration benefits they may not know about. Immigration laws change constantly, and while the potential client may not qualify for the benefit they are inquiring about, they may qualify for a different one. For example, a potential client may call to apply for a green card. Still, upon further research, an attorney may find that their estranged father was actually born in the US, and they can consequently just fill out some paperwork to claim the citizenship rights.

Visa applications and appeals typically involve the following elements.

**Visa Eligibility:** The lawyer will assess whether the client meets the eligibility criteria for the desired visa category, which can include factors such as the purpose of travel (e.g., tourism, study, work), qualifications, financial resources, ties to the home country, and compliance with immigration laws.

**Documentation:** The lawyer will evaluate the client's documentation to ensure it is complete, accurate, and supports their visa application, which may involve verifying passports, birth certificates, educational qualifications, employment records, financial statements, or any other relevant paperwork required for the specific visa category.

**Legal Compliance:** The lawyer will ensure that the client has complied with all applicable immigration laws, regulations, and procedures, which includes addressing any previous visa violations, overstays, criminal history, or other factors that may impact visa eligibility.

**Visa Denial or Revocation:** If the government denies the client's visa, the lawyer can assist in challenging the decision through the appeals process, which may involve gathering additional evidence, presenting legal arguments, or addressing any grounds for denial specified by the immigration authorities.

To determine if a potential client may have a valid visa application and appeals case, ask the following questions.

1. Are you currently in the United States? If not, when do you intend to travel to the United States?
2. Have you previously applied for a visa? If so, what was the outcome?
3. Are you aware of any reasons that may affect your eligibility for the desired visa category, such as criminal history or previous immigration violations?

4. Do you have all the necessary documentation to support your visa application?
5. Can you provide evidence of your qualifications, financial resources, or ties to your home country?
6. Have you received a visa denial or revocation? If so, do you know the grounds for the decision?
7. What is your timeline for needing the visa? Any potential travel plans?

## Visa Types

There are various visa types that a prospective client may be eligible for. Potential new clients may inquire about these visas directly or provide hints suggesting their suitability for specific visas. It's important to clarify to potential clients that only a seasoned attorney can accurately determine if they qualify for a particular visa type or any other immigration benefits. Remember this during discussions about their circumstances and preferences and while posing questions to gauge how your law firm might assist them. The following are some of the visas most frequently dealt with by immigration firms.

### WORK VISAS

A work visa is a legal authorization that allows a noncitizen to live and work in a foreign country for a specific period. It is typically issued by the host country's immigration or foreign affairs department. This type of visa is intended for individuals who have secured employment or a professional engagement in a foreign country. The requirements, validity period, and conditions for obtaining a work visa vary from country to country and often depend on the nature of the work or profession involved.

The following are a few factors you can look for.

**Eligible Occupation:** The applicant's job must fall under the categories of occupations eligible for a work visa as defined by U.S. immigration law.

**Job Offer:** The applicant must have a confirmed job offer from a U.S. employer willing to sponsor their visa application.

**Education and Experience:** The applicant should have the qualifications, skills, and experience required for the job. For certain visa categories, like the H-1B visa, a bachelor's degree or higher in the specific field is required.

**Compliance with Labor Laws:** The sponsoring employer must demonstrate compliance with U.S. labor laws, including paying prevailing wages and providing safe working conditions.

**Prevailing Wage Confirmation:** The employer must pay the foreign worker a wage equal to or greater than the prevailing wage for the occupation in the area of employment.

**No Adverse Effect:** The foreign worker's employment must not adversely affect the working conditions of similarly employed U.S. workers.

**Nonimmigrant Intent:** For nonimmigrant work visas, the applicant must demonstrate that they intend to return to their home country once their visa expires.

**Document Verification:** All documents submitted supporting the visa application must be genuine, accurate, and verifiable.

To determine if a potential client may have a valid case for a work visa, ask the following questions.

1. Have you previously applied for or been granted any type of work visa in the United States?
2. What circumstances led you to apply for a work visa?
3. Did you experience any forms of persecution or fear for your safety in your home country that are different from employment-related issues?

## U Visas

A U visa is a nonimmigrant visa for victims of certain crimes who have suffered mental or physical abuse and are helpful to law enforcement or government officials in the investigation or prosecution of criminal activity. The U visa allows these victims to remain in the U.S., work, and potentially apply for a green card. This visa strengthens the law enforcement community's ability to investigate and prosecute cases of domestic violence, sexual assault, human trafficking, and other crimes while also offering protection to victims.

Some things to look for in a strong U Visa case include the following.

**Victim of Qualifying Criminal Activity:** The applicant must have been a victim of qualifying criminal activity in the U.S. or been affected by someone who has violated U.S. laws. These crimes include, but are not limited to, domestic violence, sexual assault, trafficking, and other serious offenses.

**Suffered Substantial Physical or Mental Abuse:** The applicant must demonstrate that they have suffered substantial physical or mental abuse as a result of the crime.

**Helpful to Law Enforcement:** The applicant must be willing to assist law enforcement and government officials in investigating or prosecuting the criminal activity. They must provide a certification from a qualifying official to affirm their helpfulness.

**Admissibility to the U.S.:** The applicant must be admissible to the U.S. or obtain a waiver for any grounds of inadmissibility.

**Credible Evidence:** The applicant should have credible and consistent evidence to support their claims about the crime and its impact on them, including police reports, court documents, medical records, psychological evaluations, and personal statements.

To determine if a potential client may have a valid case for a U Visa, ask the following questions.

1. Have you been a victim of a qualifying crime in the United States?
2. Have you cooperated or assisted law enforcement in investigating or prosecuting the crime?
3. How has this crime affected your safety and well-being?

## Violence Against Women Act (VAWA) Visa

The Violence Against Women Act (VAWA) Visa in the United States is a provision that enables noncitizens who have experienced abuse from a U.S. citizen or lawful permanent resident (LPR) spouse or parent to self-petition for lawful permanent residency, also known as a green card, without the knowledge or cooperation of the abuser. The VAWA Visa is not limited by gender and extends to both women and men. Eligibility for a VAWA self-petition includes demonstrating good moral character and proving the abusive relationship. This visa aims to provide an avenue for victims of domestic violence to escape their abusive situations and secure their legal status in the U.S.

Several factors can contribute to a strong VAWA visa case that an immigration lawyer in the U.S. may handle, including the following.

**Qualifying Relationship:** The applicant must have a qualifying relationship with the abuser, who must be a U.S. citizen or LPR. The relationship can be that of a spouse, child, or parent.

**Proof of Abuse:** The applicant must provide substantial evidence of having been abused physically, sexually, or emotionally by their U.S. citizen or LPR family member.

**Residence with Abuser:** The applicant should be able to show that they lived with the abusive family member at some point.

**Good Moral Character:** The applicant needs to demonstrate good moral character, proven through police clearance records or other relevant documents.

**Impact Statement:** A strong personal declaration or impact statement detailing the abuse and its effects on the victim can significantly strengthen the case.

**Current Immigration Status:** The immigration lawyer should know the current immigration status of the client, as this can influence the strategy for the application.

To determine if a potential client may have a valid case for a VAWA, ask the following questions.

1. Have you been subjected to physical or extreme emotional abuse by a U.S. citizen or lawful permanent resident spouse or parent?

2. Have you reported this abuse or sought help from any authorities or organizations?
3. How has this abuse affected your life and safety?

## Student Visa

A student visa is a nonimmigrant visa that allows foreign individuals to study in the U.S. There are three types of student visas: F-1 for academic students enrolled in colleges, universities, high schools, language training programs, and other academic institutions; M-1 for vocational and nonacademic students; and J-1 for students in work-study based exchange visitor programs. These visas are issued to individuals accepted into a Student and Exchange Visitor Program (SEVP)-approved educational institution who can demonstrate their intent to return home after completing their studies. The visa allows the holder to stay in the U.S. for the duration of their academic program plus any authorized practical training, provided they maintain their status.

Several factors can contribute to a strong student visa case that an immigration lawyer in the U.S. may handle, including the following.

**Eligibility:** The applicant must meet the eligibility criteria for the specific student visa category, such as F-1, M-1, or J-1, including acceptance to a SEVP-approved school and must demonstrate intent to return to their home country after completing studies.

**Financial Support:** The applicant must provide proof of financial ability to cover tuition, living expenses, and other costs during their stay in the U.S.

**English Proficiency:** Applicants for student visas typically must demonstrate proficiency in English. Evidence might include test scores from an English language proficiency test such as TOEFL or IELTS.

**Academic Qualifications:** The applicant's academic record, grades, and standardized test scores will be considered. Strong academic qualifications can bolster the case.

**Honesty and Consistency:** The information provided in the application and during the consular interview should be truthful and consistent. Discrepancies can lead to visa denials.

**Preparation for the Interview:** Adequate preparation for the interview at the U.S. embassy or consulate is crucial. The applicant should be able to clearly articulate their study plans, long-term goals, and intent to return home.

For work or student visas, it can also help to ask more specific questions to qualify for that type of visa, including the following.

1. Are you applying for a work visa, student visa, or another type of visa?
2. For work visas: Did the employer fulfill sponsorship obligations? Was the client offered a job in line with visa requirements, including qualifications and wage standards?
3. For student visas: Was admission to an accredited institution secured? Were financial support and maintenance requirements met as per visa regulations?
4. Were all regulations related to work or student visas followed?

## Deportation Defense

A deportation defense case involves legal matters related to individuals facing removal or deportation from the country. Deportation occurs when immigration authorities order noncitizens to leave the United States due to violations of immigration laws, criminal convictions, or other grounds for inadmissibility. Deportation defense cases typically involve challenging the deportation order, seeking relief or protection from removal, and advocating for the individual's right to remain in the country.

Deportation defense typically involves the following elements.

**Legal Status and Eligibility:** The lawyer will assess the individual's current legal status in the United States and determine if they are eligible for any relief or protection from deportation, which can include exploring options such as asylum, cancellation of removal, adjustment of status, or waivers.

**Immigration Violations or Grounds for Removal:** The lawyer will evaluate the grounds on which the individual faces deportation and analyze the legality of the allegations, which may involve reviewing the immigration records, criminal history, or any other factors triggering the removal proceedings.

**Due Process and Procedural Rights:** The lawyer will protect the individual's due process rights throughout the deportation defense process, which includes examining any potential violations of procedural rights, such as improper notice, denial of legal representation, or failure to consider relevant evidence.

**Evidence and Documentation:** The lawyer will gather and present evidence to support the individual's case for remaining in the United States, including documentation of family ties, community involvement, employment history, contributions to society, or any other factors that demonstrate positive equities.

To determine if a potential client may have a valid deportation defense case, ask the following questions.

1. What is your current immigration status in the United States?
2. Have you received a Notice to Appear (NTA) or any other communication from immigration authorities regarding your removal proceedings?
3. Can you provide information about the grounds on which you are facing deportation?
4. Are you aware of any due process or procedural rights violations during the immigration proceedings?
5. Do you have any evidence or documentation that supports your case for remaining in the United States, such as family ties, community involvement, or employment history?
6. Have you ever applied for any relief or protection from deportation?

## Green Card Applications

A green card application case involves legal matters related to obtaining lawful permanent residency in the United States. A green card, or permanent resident card, grants a foreign national the right to live and work permanently in the U.S. These cases involve issues such as eligibility based on family ties, employment, investment, or other special categories; compliance with immigration laws; and navigating the complex application process.

Green card application cases typically have the following elements.

**Eligibility:** The lawyer will assess if the client is eligible for a green card under one of the categories specified by U.S. immigration law, which could be through family, employment, refugee or asylee status, diversity lottery, or several other special provisions.

**Compliance:** The lawyer will ensure the client has complied with all U.S. immigration laws and regulations, which includes addressing any previous visa violations, overstays, or criminal history that may impact green card eligibility.

**Documentation:** The lawyer will evaluate the client's documentation to ensure it is complete, accurate, and supports their green card application. This may involve verifying passports, birth certificates, marriage certificates, employment records, financial statements, or any other required paperwork.

**Application Process:** The lawyer will guide the client through the complex green card application process, which can include multiple steps such as filing petitions, attending interviews, undergoing medical examinations, and responding to requests for evidence.

To determine if a potential client may have a valid green card application case, ask the following questions.

1. What is your current immigration status in the United States?
2. Under which category are you planning to apply for a green card–family, employment, refugee or asylee status, diversity lottery, etc.?
3. Have you ever violated any U.S. immigration laws, overstayed a visa, or have any criminal history?
4. Do you have all the necessary documentation to support your green card application?
5. Have you started the green card application process? If so, what stage are you currently at?

## Asylum Applications

An asylum application case involves legal matters related to individuals seeking protection from persecution or fear of persecution in their home country. The government grants asylum to people who have suffered persecution or fear that they will suffer it due to race, religion, nationality, membership in a particular social group, or political opinion. These cases rely on proving the credibility of the individual's fear, demonstrating their situation's severity, and navigating the complex asylum application process.

Asylum application cases typically involve the following elements.

**Credibility:** The lawyer will assess whether the client can provide a credible and consistent account of their fear of persecution, which can involve evaluating their testimony, supporting documents, and any other evidence corroborating their claims.

**Persecution or Fear of Persecution:** The lawyer will examine the nature and severity of the persecution or fear of it, which may include reviewing evidence of past harm, threats, or other forms of mistreatment based on race, religion, nationality, membership in a particular social group, or political opinion.

**Eligibility for Asylum:** The lawyer will ensure that the client meets the eligibility criteria for asylum, which includes factors such as filing within one year of arrival in the U.S. unless exceptions apply, not being firmly resettled in another country, and not being subject to certain bars to asylum.

**Application Process:** The lawyer will guide the client through the complex asylum application process, which includes preparing and filing the application, attending interviews and court hearings, and responding to requests for evidence.

To determine if a potential client may have a valid asylum application case, ask the following questions.

1.  Can you describe the persecution or fear you will face in your home country?

2. Can you provide evidence or documentation to support your claims of persecution or fear of persecution?
3. When did you arrive in the United States? Have you filed an asylum application within one year of your arrival?
4. Have you resided in other countries before coming to the United States? If so, did you apply for asylum there?
5. Are you aware of any reasons that might bar you from receiving asylum in the United States?

## Environmental Law

Environmental law cases involve legal matters related to protecting the environment, natural resources, and public health. They often revolve around compliance with environmental regulations, enforcement of environmental rights, and resolution of disputes involving pollution, land use, wildlife protection, waste management, and other environmental issues. The following are the main elements of an environmental law case.

**Regulatory Compliance:** These cases often involve businesses or individuals who must ensure compliance with local, state, and federal environmental laws and regulations. These can include matters related to emissions, waste disposal, hazardous materials, water quality, and other environmental standards.

**Enforcement Actions:** Environmental law cases can involve defending against enforcement actions brought by government agencies for alleged violations of environmental laws, which can include penalties, injunctions, cleanup orders, and other enforcement measures.

**Land Use and Zoning:** These cases can involve disputes over land use and zoning laws that govern how the land can be used and developed, including construction, development, conservation, and other land-use matters.

**Litigation and Dispute Resolution:** Environmental law cases can involve litigation and dispute resolution over environmental harm, property damage, personal injury, and other issues related to environmental impact.

To qualify leads for environmental law cases, ask the following questions.

1. What environmental issues are you facing—regulatory compliance, enforcement action, land use dispute, etc.?
2. Have you received any notices, citations, or enforcement actions from government agencies related to environmental laws?
3. Are you involved in any disputes or litigation related to environmental harm, property damage, or other environmental impacts?
4. Do you need guidance on compliance with environmental regulations for your business operations or activities?
5. Are you facing any land use, zoning, construction, or development challenges that may have environmental implications?

## Pollution Cases

A pollution case involves legal matters related to the contamination of the environment, including air, water, soil, and noise pollution. These cases often revolve around violations of environmental laws and regulations, harm caused by pollution, and disputes over liability and damages.

Pollution cases typically involve the following elements.

**Regulatory Violations:** The lawyer will examine whether there have been violations of local, state, or federal environmental laws and regulations, which could involve unauthorized emissions or discharges, failure to obtain necessary permits, noncompliance with regulatory standards, and other breaches of environmental law.

**Harm Caused by Pollution:** The lawyer will assess whether the pollution has caused harm to the environment, public health, property, or other legally protected interests. This can involve reviewing scientific evidence, medical reports, property damage assessments, and other relevant documentation.

**Liability and Damages:** The lawyer will evaluate who is responsible for the pollution and what damages may be recoverable. This can involve identifying potential defendants, assessing their role in causing the pollution, and calculating the damages the client can claim.

**Legal Remedies:** The lawyer will explore what legal remedies are available, including enforcement actions, injunctions, compensation for damages, cleanup orders, and other forms of relief.

To determine if a potential client may have a valid pollution case, ask the following questions.

1. Can you describe the nature of the pollution issue you are facing—air, water, soil, noise, etc.?
2. Do you believe there have been violations of environmental laws or regulations? If so, can you provide more details?
3. Has the pollution caused harm to the environment, public health, your property, or other interests? Can you provide any evidence or documentation to support this?
4. Are you aware of who might be responsible for the pollution? If so, can you provide more details?
5. What kind of resolution are you seeking—enforcement action, compensation for damages, cleanup order, etc.?

## Natural Resource Management

A natural resource management case involves legal matters related to managing and conserving natural resources such as water, land, minerals, forests, wildlife, and fisheries. These cases often revolve around land use, water rights, mineral extraction, wildlife protection, forestry management, and fishing regulations.

Natural resource management cases typically involve the following elements.

**Regulatory Compliance:** The lawyer will assess whether there have been any violations of local, state, or federal natural resource laws and regulations, which could involve unauthorized use or extraction of resources, noncompliance with conservation measures, and other breaches of law.

**Disputes over Resource Use:** The lawyer will examine whether there are disputes over the use or ownership of natural resources, which can involve conflicts between different users, claims of property damage or environmental harm, and other disputes.

**Conservation and Sustainability Issues:** The lawyer will evaluate whether there are issues related to the conservation and sustainable use of natural resources, which can involve reviewing scientific evidence, assessing the impact of activities on the environment and biodiversity, and other considerations.

**Legal Remedies:** The lawyer will explore what legal remedies are available, including enforcement actions, injunctions, compensation for damages, orders for restoration or remediation, and other forms of relief.

To determine if a potential client may have a valid natural resource management case, ask the following questions.

1. Can you describe the nature of the natural resource issue you face—water, land, minerals, forests, wildlife, fisheries, etc.?
2. Do you believe there have been violations of natural resource laws or regulations? If so, can you provide more details?
3. Are you involved in disputes over using or owning natural resources? Can you provide any evidence or documentation to support this?
4. Are you facing any issues related to the conservation and sustainable use of natural resources? If so, can you provide more details?
5. What kind of resolution are you seeking—enforcement action, compensation for damages, order for restoration or remediation, etc.?

## Regulatory Compliance

A regulatory compliance case involves legal matters related to ensuring that businesses or individuals adhere to all relevant local, state, and federal laws and regulations. These cases often revolve around environmental regulations, health and safety standards, financial regulations, data protection laws, and other regulatory requirements.

Regulatory compliance cases typically involve the following elements.

**Clear Violations:** The lawyer will assess whether there have been clear violations of any laws or regulations, which could involve breaches of environmental standards, noncompliance with health and safety requirements, failure to meet financial regulations, and other breaches of law.

**Impact of Violations:** The lawyer will examine the impact of these violations, which can involve reviewing potential harm to the public, damage to the environment, financial losses, and other consequences of non-compliance.

**Potential Remedies:** The lawyer will consider what remedies may be available. This could involve actions to ensure future compliance, penalties for past violations, orders for remediation, and other forms of relief.

**Willingness to Comply:** A suitable case often involves a client who acknowledges the issue and is willing to take steps to achieve compliance.

To determine if a potential client may have a valid regulatory compliance case, ask the following questions.

1. Can you describe the nature of the regulatory compliance issue you face?
2. Do you believe there have been violations of any specific laws or regulations? If so, can you provide more details?
3. What is the impact of these alleged violations? Have there been any consequences such as fines, penalties, orders for remediation, etc.?
4. Are you willing to take steps to ensure future compliance with these laws or regulations?
5. What kind of resolution are you seeking—actions to ensure future compliance, penalties for past violations, orders for remediation, etc.?

## Environmental Litigation

Environmental litigation involves legal disputes related to the environment, including pollution, land use, natural resource extraction, wildlife protection, and compliance with environmental laws and regulations. These cases often involve private parties, government agencies, and nonprofit organizations.

Environmental litigation cases typically involve the following elements.

**Regulatory Violations:** The lawyer will examine whether there have been violations of local, state, or federal environmental laws and regulations, which could involve unauthorized emissions or discharges, failure to obtain necessary permits, noncompliance with regulatory standards, and other breaches of environmental law.

**Tangible Environmental Harm:** The lawyer will assess whether the alleged actions have caused actual harm to the environment, public health, property, or other legally protected interests. This can involve reviewing scientific evidence, medical reports, property damage assessments, and other relevant documentation.

**Clear Liability:** The lawyer will evaluate who is responsible for the alleged harm and whether liability is established based on available evidence.

**Available Legal Remedies:** The lawyer will explore available legal remedies, including enforcement actions, injunctions to stop harmful activities, compensation for damages, cleanup orders, and other forms of relief.

To determine if a potential client may have a valid environmental litigation case, ask the following questions.

1. Can you describe the nature of your environmental issue?
2. Do you believe there have been violations of environmental laws or regulations? If so, can you provide more details?
3. Has the alleged action caused tangible harm to the environment, public health, or your property? Can you give any evidence or documentation to support this?
4. Are you aware of who might be responsible for the alleged harm? If so, can you provide more details?
5. What kind of resolution are you seeking—enforcement action, injunction, compensation for damages, cleanup order, etc.?

# Estate Planning

An estate planning case involves legal matters related to managing and transferring a person's assets upon death or incapacitation. Estate planning ensures that an individual's wishes regarding their assets are respected and carried out while minimizing taxes and avoiding probate where possible.

## CRITICAL COMPONENTS OF ESTATE PLANNING

**Wills:** A will is a legal document that outlines how to distribute an individual's assets upon death. It can also specify guardianship for minor children.

**Trusts**: Trusts are legal arrangements that allow a third party or trustee to hold assets on behalf of a beneficiary. Trusts can help avoid probate, reduce estate taxes, and provide for beneficiaries.

**Estate Taxes:** Estate tax planning involves strategies to minimize the impact of state and federal inheritance taxes.

**Power of Attorney:** This document allows individuals to appoint someone to manage their financial affairs if they cannot.

**Healthcare Directives:** These documents specify an individual's wishes for medical treatment if they cannot decide for themself.

To qualify leads for estate planning cases, ask the following questions.

1. Do you currently have a will or any trusts established?
2. Are you concerned about estate taxes or probate issues?
3. Do you have designated individuals to manage your financial and healthcare decisions if you cannot?
4. Are there specific wishes or concerns you have about the distribution of your assets?
5. Do you have complex family or financial situations, such as children from multiple marriages, ownership of a business, or substantial retirement assets?

## Wills and Trusts

A will and trust case involves legal matters related to the creation, management, and execution of wills and trusts. A will is a legal document outlining how individuals want their assets distributed upon death. On the other hand, a trust is a legal arrangement where one party (the trustee) holds assets for the benefit of another party (the beneficiary).

Will and trust cases typically involve the following elements.

**Drafting and Execution:** The client needs assistance drafting a will or setting up a trust. The lawyer can help ensure the documents are legally valid and accurately reflect the client's wishes.

**Asset Complexity:** The client must manage or distribute substantial or complex assets, including businesses, real estate, investments, and other property types.

**Family Dynamics:** The client has complicated family situations, such as multiple marriages, blended families, minor children, or estranged relatives that require careful estate planning.

**Tax Planning:** The client wants to minimize estate taxes or avoid probate by using trusts and other estate planning strategies.

**Disputes:** The client is involved in a dispute over a will or trust, such as a contest over the validity of a will, disagreements among beneficiaries, or issues with the performance of a trustee.

To determine if a potential client may have a valid will and trust case, ask the following questions.

1. Do you currently have a will or any trusts set up? Do you feel they accurately reflect your wishes and meet your needs?
2. Can you describe the nature and extent of your assets? Do you own a business, real estate, or other substantial assets?
3. Can you tell me about your family situation? Do you have multiple marriages, blended families, minor children, or other family dynamics that may affect your estate planning?
4. Are you concerned about estate taxes or probate issues? Are you interested in strategies to minimize taxes or avoid probate?

5. Are you involved in any disputes over a will or trust? Can you provide more details about these issues?

## Probate Administration

Probate administration involves the legal process of managing and distributing a deceased person's estate according to their will or, if no will exists, according to state law. A probate court oversees this process and often involves identifying and inventorying the deceased's assets, paying debts and taxes, and distributing the remaining assets to heirs or beneficiaries.

Probate administration cases typically involve the following elements.

**Valid Will:** The deceased left a valid will that clearly outlines how they wanted their assets distributed. Disputes can arise if there are questions about the will's validity or terms.

**Estate Complexity:** The deceased had substantial or complex assets that must be managed and distributed, including businesses, real estate, investments, and other property types.

**Debts and Taxes:** The estate has significant debts or tax obligations that must be handled properly.

**Disputes:** Family members or other potential heirs are disputing the will or the distribution of assets.

**No Will:** The deceased did not leave a will, requiring the estate to be divided according to state law.

To determine if a potential client may have a valid probate administration case, ask the following questions.

1. Did the deceased leave a will? If so, is there any dispute about its validity or its terms?
2. Can you describe the nature and extent of the deceased's assets? Did they own a business, real estate, or other substantial assets?
3. Are there significant debts or taxes that must be paid from the estate?

4. Are there any disputes among family members or other potential heirs about the will or the distribution of assets?
5. Are you familiar with your state's laws about dividing assets if the deceased did not leave a will?

## Estate Tax Planning

Estate tax planning involves creating strategies to minimize estate taxes upon an individual's death. This area of law is crucial because without careful planning, a significant portion of one's estate could go to taxes rather than beneficiaries. An estate tax planning case arises when an individual has substantial assets and seeks legal advice to structure their estate strategically to reduce or eliminate estate tax liabilities.

Estate tax planning cases typically involve the following.

**High Net Worth:** The individual has substantial assets that could be subject to estate taxes. As of 2023, the federal estate tax applies to estates worth more than $11.7 million for individuals and $23.4 million for couples.

**Asset Complexity:** The estate includes various assets, such as real estate, businesses, investments, and retirement accounts that require sophisticated planning strategies.

**Family Considerations:** The individual has specific wishes regarding the distribution of their assets among family members, charities, or other beneficiaries.

**Business Succession:** The individual owns a business and needs to plan for its transition after their death.

To determine if a potential client may have a valid estate tax planning case, ask the following questions.

1. Can you estimate your total estate value? Is it likely to exceed the federal estate tax exemption limit?
2. Can you describe the types of assets included in your estate? Do you own a business, real estate, or other significant investments?
3. Do you have specific wishes for distributing your assets after your death?

4. Are you concerned about the potential impact of estate taxes on your heirs?
5. If you own a business, have you planned its succession?

## Guardianship and Conservatorship

Guardianship and conservatorship cases involve legal processes where a court appoints an individual (the guardian or conservator) to make decisions for another person who cannot do so because of age, illness, or disability. A guardian generally makes personal decisions for the ward, such as healthcare and living arrangements, while a conservator manages the ward's financial affairs.

Guardianship and conservatorship cases involve the following elements.

**Incapacity:** There is clear evidence that the person (the proposed ward) cannot make sound decisions due to age, illness, or disability.

**Assets:** The proposed ward has assets that require management or protection.

**Disputes:** There are disagreements among family members or other interested parties about who should be appointed guardian or conservator or how the ward's affairs should be managed.

**Welfare Concerns:** There are concerns about the proposed ward's welfare, such as potential neglect, abuse, or exploitation.

**Complex Needs:** The proposed ward has complex medical, emotional, or financial needs that require professional management.

To determine if a potential client may have a valid guardianship or conservatorship case, ask the following questions.

1. Can you describe the condition of the person for whom you're seeking guardianship or conservatorship? What evidence do you have of their inability to make decisions?
2. Does the proposed ward have assets that need management?
3. Are there any disputes among family members or others about who should be appointed guardian or conservator or how to manage the ward's affairs?

4. Are there concerns about the proposed ward's welfare, such as potential neglect, abuse, or exploitation?
5. Does the proposed ward have complex needs that require professional management?

## Health Law

Health law encompasses various legal issues related to healthcare, including healthcare policy, regulations, and practices. A health law case could involve various sectors such as hospitals, pharmaceutical companies, insurance firms, individual practitioners, and patients.

The following are key areas where legal disputes often arise with regard to health law.

**Medical Malpractice:** These cases involve allegations of negligence by healthcare providers leading to patient harm or injury and could include misdiagnosis, surgical errors, medication errors, etc.

**Insurance Disputes:** These cases typically involve disagreements over coverage between patients or care providers and health insurers.

**Regulatory Compliance:** These cases involve healthcare entities facing legal issues related to compliance with federal and state health laws, such as the Health Insurance Portability and Accountability Act (HIPAA), the Affordable Care Act (ACA), etc.

**Fraud and Abuse:** These cases often involve allegations of fraud or abuse within the healthcare system, such as billing for services not rendered, kickbacks, or upcoding.

**Patient Rights:** These cases involve legal issues related to patient rights, such as informed consent, privacy, and access to medical records.

To qualify leads for health law cases, ask potential clients the following questions.

1. Are you seeking representation for a medical malpractice claim? If so, can you provide details about the alleged negligence and the harm or injury you suffered?
2. Do you have a dispute with your health insurance company over coverage or reimbursement?
3. Are you a healthcare provider or entity facing issues related to regulatory compliance? If so, what specific regulations are involved?
4. Are you facing allegations of fraud or abuse within the health-care system? Can you provide details about the allegations?
5. Do you believe your rights as a patient have been violated? If so, can you provide details about the alleged violation?

## Medical Malpractice Defense

Medical malpractice defense cases involve defending healthcare providers or medical institutions accused of negligence resulting in harm or injury to a patient. Medical malpractice defense typically involves the following.

**Strong Evidence:** There is strong evidence that the healthcare provider adhered to the standard of care, meaning they provided the level and type of care that a reasonably competent and skilled healthcare professional with a similar background and in the same medical community would have provided under the circumstances.

**Causation:** There is a strong argument that any harm or injury suffered by the patient was not directly caused by the healthcare provider's actions or omissions.

**Expert Testimony:** The defense can produce expert witnesses to testify to the healthcare provider's adherence to the standard of care and/or that the healthcare provider's actions did not cause harm or injury.

**Damage Assessment:** The alleged damages claimed by the plaintiff—financial, physical, emotional—are arguable and can be minimized.

To determine if a potential client may have a valid medical malpractice defense case, ask the following questions.

1. Can you provide details about the alleged malpractice and the harm or injury suffered by the patient?
2. Do you believe you adhered to the standard of care in treating the patient? If so, can you explain how?
3. Can you argue that your actions or omissions did not directly cause the patient's harm or injury? If so, can you provide details?
4. Can experts testify to your adherence to the standard of care and/or that your actions did not cause the patient harm or injury?
5. Can you provide information about the damages claimed by the plaintiff?

## Healthcare Regulatory Compliance

Healthcare regulatory compliance cases involve legal matters related to adherence to healthcare laws, regulations, and standards set by federal and state authorities. These could include laws like the Health Insurance Portability and Accountability Act (HIPAA), the Affordable Care Act (ACA), the False Claims Act, the Anti-Kickback Statute, and more.

Healthcare regulatory compliance cases typically involve the following.

**Clear Compliance Issue:** There is a clear issue of noncompliance with healthcare regulations that needs to be addressed.

**Potential or Actual Enforcement Action:** The healthcare provider or entity is facing potential or actual enforcement action from regulatory authorities.

**Complexity:** The case involves complex legal or factual issues that require expert legal analysis and advice.

**Significant Consequences:** The potential consequences of noncompliance are significant, such as substantial fines, penalties, or loss of license.

**Need for Policy Development or Revision:** The healthcare provider or entity needs assistance in developing or revising policies and procedures to ensure regulatory compliance.

To determine if a potential client may have a valid healthcare regulatory compliance case, ask the following questions.

1. Can you explain the specific compliance issue you're facing? What healthcare laws or regulations are involved?
2. Are you facing potential or actual enforcement action from regulatory authorities? If so, can you provide details?
3. Does your case involve complex legal or factual issues that you believe require expert legal analysis and advice?
4. What are the potential consequences if you're found to be noncompliant?
5. Do you need assistance developing or revising policies and procedures to ensure regulatory compliance?

## Healthcare Contracts and Transactions

Healthcare contracts and transaction cases typically involve legal matters related to the negotiation, drafting, and execution of various types of agreements within the healthcare industry. These can include contracts between healthcare providers and hospitals, agreements with insurance companies, acquisition and merger agreements, joint venture agreements, employment contracts, and more.

Healthcare contracts and transaction cases typically involve the following.

**Significant Deal Value:** This involves a contract or transaction with significant financial implications.

**Complexity:** The case involves complex contractual terms, legal issues, or regulatory considerations that require expert legal analysis and advice.

**Risk of Dispute:** There's a potential risk of dispute or litigation over the contract or transaction.

**Need for Negotiation:** The client needs assistance negotiating favorable contract or transaction terms.

**Regulatory Compliance:** The contract or transaction must comply with specific healthcare laws and regulations.

To determine if a potential client may have a valid healthcare contract and transactions case, ask the following questions.

1. Can you provide details about the contract or transaction you're involved with? What is its financial value?
2. Does your case involve complex contractual terms, legal issues, or regulatory considerations?
3. Is there a potential risk of dispute or litigation over the contract or transaction?
4. Do you need assistance negotiating the contract or transaction terms?
5. Are there specific healthcare laws and regulations that the contract or transaction must comply with?

## HIPAA Compliance

HIPAA compliance cases typically involve legal matters related to adherence to the Health Insurance Portability and Accountability Act (HIPAA). HIPAA is a federal law requiring national standards to protect sensitive patient health information from being disclosed without the patient's consent or knowledge.

HIPAA compliance cases involve the following.

**Clear Compliance Issue:** A clear issue of noncompliance with HIPAA regulations needs to be addressed.

**Potential or Actual Enforcement Action:** The healthcare provider or entity faces potential or actual enforcement action from regulatory authorities such as the Office for Civil Rights (OCR).

**Breach of Patient Information:** A protected health information (PHI) breach could potentially lead to penalties.

**Need for Policy Development or Revision:** The healthcare provider or entity needs assistance developing or revising policies and procedures to ensure HIPAA compliance.

**Training and Education:** The healthcare provider or entity must train staff to understand and comply with HIPAA regulations.

To determine if a potential client may have a valid HIPAA compliance case, ask the following questions.

1. Can you explain the specific compliance issue you're facing? What aspects of HIPAA are involved?
2. Are you facing potential or actual enforcement action from regulatory authorities? If so, can you provide details?
3. Has there been a breach of protected health information? If so, can you provide details?
4. Do you need assistance developing or revising policies and procedures to ensure HIPAA compliance?
5. Does your staff require training to understand and comply with HIPAA regulations?

## Tax Law

A tax law case typically involves legal issues related to interpreting and applying federal, state, or local tax laws. These cases can range from individual income tax issues to corporate tax matters, estate tax planning, or even disputes with the Internal Revenue Service (IRS) or state tax authorities.

The following are the two types of tax law cases.

**Tax Planning**: These involve proactive legal advice to help individuals or businesses minimize their tax liability within the bounds of the law, which could include strategies for income tax, estate tax, business tax, and more.

**Tax Disputes**: A disagreement between the taxpayer and the tax authorities falls into this category. The disagreement could be about the amount of tax due, penalties imposed, or even the interpretation of tax laws.

Tax law cases typically involve the following.

**Potential or Actual Dispute**: The taxpayer faces a potential or actual dispute with the IRS or state tax authorities.

**Need for Planning**: The client needs assistance with tax planning to minimize future tax liability.

**Criminal Charges**: In extreme cases, the taxpayer may face criminal charges related to tax evasion or fraud.

To determine if a potential client may have a valid tax law case, ask the following questions.

1.  Can you explain the specific tax issue you're facing? What types of taxes are involved—income, estate, business, etc.?
2.  Are you facing a potential or actual dispute with the IRS or state tax authorities? If so, can you provide details?
3.  Are you seeking assistance with tax planning to minimize future tax liability? If so, can you provide details about your financial situation?
4.  Are you facing any criminal charges related to tax evasion or fraud?

## Tax Planning and Advice

Tax planning and advice cases typically involve legal guidance on effectively managing tax obligations. This includes understanding tax laws, structuring financial transactions and business decisions tax-efficiently, estate planning, retirement planning, and more.

Tax planning and advice cases typically involve the following.

**High Financial Stakes**: The client has substantial assets, high income, or complex financial scenarios that could significantly benefit from strategic tax planning.

**Business Ownership**: The client owns a business and needs advice on tax-efficiently structuring business transactions.

**Estate Planning Needs**: The client wishes to pass on significant assets to heirs and needs advice on minimizing estate taxes.

**Retirement Planning**: The client plans for retirement and needs advice on optimizing their tax situation.

**International Considerations**: The client has financial interests in other countries and needs advice on managing international tax obligations.

To determine if a potential client may have a valid tax planning and advice case, ask the following questions.

1. Can you provide details about your financial situation? Do you have substantial assets, high income, or complex financial scenarios?
2. Do you own a business? Are you looking for advice on tax-efficient business practices?
3. Are you looking for advice on estate planning to minimize estate taxes?
4. Are you planning for retirement and need advice on optimizing your tax situation?
5. Do you have any financial interests in other countries?

## Tax Disputes and Litigation

Tax disputes and litigation cases typically involve legal disagreements between taxpayers and the IRS or state tax authorities. These could involve audits, appeals, tax collection disputes, or allegations of tax fraud.

Tax disputes and litigation cases involve the following.

**Disagreements with the IRS or State Tax Authorities**: The taxpayer disagrees with the assessment or decision made by the IRS or state tax authorities and wishes to challenge it.

**Audits**: The IRS or state tax authorities audit the taxpayer and require legal representation.

**Tax Collection Disputes**: The taxpayer disputes the amount of tax claimed by the tax authorities or the collection method.

**Allegations of Tax Fraud**: The taxpayer is accused of tax fraud and needs legal defense.

To determine if a potential client may have a valid tax dispute and litigation case, ask the following questions.

1. Are you currently disagreeing with the IRS or state tax authorities? If so, can you provide details about the nature of the dispute?

2. Are you currently being audited by the IRS or state tax authorities?
3. Do you dispute the amount of tax claimed by the tax authorities or their collection method? If so, can you provide details?
4. Are you facing allegations of tax fraud?

## IRS Audits and Appeals

IRS audits and appeals cases involve situations where a taxpayer's tax return is selected for review by the IRS to verify that income, deductions, and credits are reported accurately. If the taxpayer disagrees with the audit findings, they can appeal the decision within the IRS or in court.

IRS audits and appeals cases involve the following.

**Complexity**: The audit involves complex tax issues or large amounts of money.

**Disagreement with Audit Findings**: The taxpayer disagrees with the findings and wishes to challenge them.

**Potential Penalties**: The taxpayer may face significant penalties or additional tax liability due to the audit.

**Criminal Charges**: In extreme cases, the audit may lead to allegations of tax fraud or evasion, which could result in criminal charges.

To determine if a potential client may have a valid case for IRS audits and appeals, ask the following questions.

1. Have you been selected for an IRS audit? If so, can you provide details about the nature of the audit and the issues involved?
2. Do you disagree with the findings of the audit? If so, why?
3. Are you facing potential penalties or additional tax liability due to the audit?
4. Are you facing any criminal charges related to the audit?

## Estate and Gift Tax Planning

Estate and gift tax planning cases typically involve legal guidance related to transferring wealth during a person's life (gifts) or after death (estate). These cases often focus on minimizing the tax burden of these transfers to maximize the amount that goes to the intended recipients.

Estate and gift tax planning cases typically involve the following.

**High Net Worth**: The client has substantial assets that could be subject to estate or gift taxes.

**Complex Family or Financial Situations**: The client has a complex family situation (e.g., multiple marriages, children from different relationships) or complex financial scenarios (e.g., owning a business, having assets in multiple jurisdictions) that require careful planning.

**Charitable Giving**: The client wishes to make significant charitable gifts that need to be structured in a tax-efficient manner.

**International Considerations**: The client has assets in other countries or beneficiaries who are not U.S. citizens or residents, which can complicate estate and gift tax planning.

To determine if a potential client may have a valid Estate and gift tax planning case, ask the following questions:

1. Can you provide details about your financial situation? Do you have substantial assets that could be subject to estate or gift taxes?
2. Can you describe your family situation? Are there any complexities (e.g., multiple marriages, children from different relationships) that might affect estate or gift tax planning?
3. Are you planning to make significant charitable gifts? If so, have you considered how to do this tax-efficiently?
4. Do you have assets in other countries, or are any of your intended beneficiaries, not U.S. citizens or residents?

## Insurance Law

Insurance law cases typically involve disputes between insurance companies and policyholders over the terms and conditions of insurance policies, coverage issues, or claim settlements. These can fall under various categories, including health, auto, life, homeowners, commercial liability, and more.

The following is an overview.

**Policy Disputes**: These involve disagreements over interpreting policy terms and conditions. The policyholder may believe that a specific event or damage should be covered, while the insurer disagrees.

**Bad Faith Claims**: These occur when an insurance company is accused of not handling a claim fairly and honestly. Examples could include denying a claim without a valid reason, failing to investigate a claim promptly, or not settling a claim when liability is clear.

**Coverage Disputes**: These involve disagreements over whether a specific event or damage is covered under the policy's terms.

**Claim Settlement Disputes**: These occur when the policyholder disagrees with the amount offered by the insurer to settle a claim.

To qualify leads for these cases, ask potential clients the following questions.

1. Can you describe the nature of your dispute with your insurance company? Is it related to policy terms, claim settlement, or coverage?
2. Do you believe the insurance company has acted in bad faith? If so, can you provide specific examples of their actions?
3. Have you received a formal claim denial from the insurance company? If so, on what grounds have they denied it?
4. Do you disagree with the amount the insurance company offers to settle your claim?

## Insurance Coverage Disputes

Insurance coverage disputes typically arise when an insurance company denies a claim, arguing that the event or damage in question is not covered under the policy terms. These cases require interpretation of the policy's language and an examination of the circumstances surrounding the claim.

Insurance coverage dispute cases typically involve the following.

**Clear Policy Language**: The policy language supports the policyholder's claim that the event or damage should be covered.

**Significant Damages**: The claim involves significant potential damages or financial loss for the policyholder.

**Bad Faith**: There is evidence that the insurance company has acted in bad faith, such as denying a claim without a valid reason or failing to investigate the claim properly.

To determine if a potential client may have a valid Insurance coverage dispute case, ask the following questions.

1. Can you provide details about your insurance policy and the claim you filed?
2. Has the insurance company denied your claim? If so, on what grounds?
3. Do you believe the policy language supports your claim that the insurance company should cover the damage?
4. What are the potential damages or financial losses involved in your claim?
5. Do you believe the insurance company has acted in bad faith?

## Bad Faith Claims

Bad faith claims cases typically involve accusations against insurance companies for not handling a claim fairly and honestly. Bad faith can occur in numerous ways, such as denying a claim without a valid reason, undervaluing a claim, failing to investigate a claim promptly, or not settling a claim when liability is clear.

Bad faith claims cases involve the following.

**Clear Evidence of Bad Faith**: The policyholder can provide specific examples of bad faith actions by the insurance company, such as unreasonably delaying payment, failing to conduct a thorough investigation, or refusing to pay a claim without a valid reason.

**Significant Damages**: The policyholder has suffered substantial financial harm due to the insurance company's bad-faith actions.

**Violation of State Laws**: The insurance company's actions violate state-specific insurance laws, which vary across the U.S.

To determine if a potential client may have a valid bad faith claims case, ask the following questions.

1. Can you provide specific examples of actions by the insurance company you believe were conducted in bad faith?
2. How has the insurance company's handling of your claim caused you financial harm?
3. Have you received a formal claim denial from the insurance company? If so, on what grounds have they denied it?
4. Were there any delays in the claim process? If yes, how long were the delays? How did the insurance company justify them?

## Subrogation

In the context of insurance law, subrogation refers to the right of an insurance company to recover the number of claims paid to a policyholder from a third party that caused the loss. For example, if you are involved in a car accident caused by another driver and your insurer pays for your repairs, your insurer may then pursue recovery of these costs from the at-fault driver or their insurer. These questions can help a salesperson assess whether the potential client's situation could lead to a successful subrogation case. Suppose the answers suggest clear liability, recoverable damages, and solvency of the third party. In that case, it suggests that the case may be worth pursuing with a lawyer specialized in subrogation cases.

Subrogation cases typically involve the following.

**Clear Liability**: The third party's liability can be proven.

**Recoverable Damages**: Significant damages can be recovered from the third party or their insurer.

**Solvency of the Third Party**: Third parties can pay through their resources or insurance coverage.

To determine if a potential client may have a valid subrogation case, ask the following questions.

1. Can you describe the incident that led to your loss? Who was at fault?
2. Has your insurance company compensated you for your loss?
3. Is there clear evidence that the third party is liable for the loss?
4. Did the third party have insurance during the incident? If so, do you know the details of their coverage?
5. What is the estimated amount of your loss?

## Policy Interpretation

Policy interpretation cases involve disputes over the language and terms of an insurance policy. These cases arise when a policyholder and their insurance company disagree on how a policy should be interpreted, often about whether a specific event or damage is covered. Suppose the policy language is ambiguous. Significant damages and precedent cases may favor the policyholder. In that case, the case may be worth pursuing with a lawyer specialized in policy interpretation cases.

Policy interpretation cases typically involve the following.

**Ambiguous Policy Language**: The policy contains language that can be reasonably interpreted in multiple ways.

**Significant Damages**: The claim involves consequential potential damages or financial loss for the policyholder.

**Precedent Cases**: There are previous similar cases where courts have interpreted the policy language in favor of the policyholder.

To determine if a potential client may have a valid policy interpretation case, ask the following questions.

1. Can you provide details about your insurance policy and the claim you filed?
2. Has the insurance company denied your claim? If so, on what grounds?
3. Could the policy language be clearer concerning your claim?
4. What are the potential damages or financial losses involved in your claim?
5. Are you aware of any similar cases where the policy language was interpreted in favor of the policyholder?

# CHAPTER 16

# Summarizing Sales for Law Firms

In *Connect Convert,* we've outlined a comprehensive set of strategies designed to transform lawyers and their teams into law firm sales machines. While many law firms focus on growing by generating leads through marketing efforts, the true potential for firm growth and client satisfaction lies in how the firm serves its leads and customers. The development and implementation of a powerful, well-designed system to engage these leads effectively as described in this book can be a game changer.

You should focus on attracting leads through marketing efforts and recognize that the real magic happens in the stages that follow. Use the insights in this book to develop a robust, meticulously crafted system for engaging with your potential new customers and leads. Focus on connecting with them on a personal level, understanding their needs, and demonstrating how your services offer the optimal solution. That truly sets the stage for growth.

This book emphasizes the importance of not just any follow-up, but a powerful, systematic approach to turning initial interest into concrete, signed cases. It's about building a framework that doesn't just aim for conversion but nurtures a relationship that extends far beyond the signing of documents. These interactions are tailored to leave lasting impressions, transforming clients into more than just case numbers; they become advocates for your firm. The satisfaction and trust developed through this process encourage them to become invaluable referral sources, sharing their positive experiences with others and thereby organically growing your firm's reputation and client base.

*Connect Convert* addresses the fact that creating an ecosystem within your firm where every team member, from the front desk to the senior partners, plays a crucial role in the client conversion process. By fostering a culture that prioritizes empathy, responsiveness, and expertise, you ensure that every touchpoint with a potential client reinforces their decision to choose your services. This holistic approach to growth—combining strategic marketing to attract leads, followed by a powerful system for connection and conversion—is what truly distinguishes the most successful firms in the competitive landscape of the legal industry.

## Sustaining Success

Applying the concepts and techniques outlined in this book is not an overnight task. It requires dedication, continuous practice, and sometimes a willingness to evolve aspects of your personality. To truly integrate these strategies into your daily practice, anticipate revisiting this guide frequently. Track your performance often and celebrate your successes in getting better every day at applying what you learned.

Implementing a buddy system is an effective strategy to reinforce accountability and support as you apply the insights gained from your learning endeavors. By pairing up with a colleague, peer, or friend who shares similar goals or challenges, you create a mutually beneficial relationship where both parties are committed to monitoring progress, providing honest feedback, and encouraging each other through setbacks and successes. This collaborative approach not only helps in maintaining motivation but also fosters a sense of camaraderie and shared purpose.

Discussing applications of new strategies, troubleshooting problems together, and celebrating achievements can greatly enhance the retention and practical implementation of newly acquired knowledge can make a huge difference. Having someone to regularly check-in with helps ensure that both individuals remain focused and proactive in their commitment to applying and integrating these lessons into their professional lives, thereby maximizing the impact of their learning. Plus it can be a lot more fun if you find a buddy that is truly committed to giving you positive feedback and support.

In addition to self-directed learning, consider seeking personalized coaching. Depending on your specific areas of improvement, you may benefit from personalized coaching from a sales coach, a mindset coach, NLP coach or other personal coach. Find a personalized coach who can tailor the learning experience in this book to your unique needs, strengths, and areas for development, offering targeted strategies and support that can dramatically accelerate your progress.

Depending on your specific goals and challenges, a range of coaches can provide invaluable assistance, each bringing a unique skill set to address various aspects of personal and professional development. Following are a few coach types you may wish to consider working with.

**Sales Coach**: Specializes in enhancing your sales skills and strategies, refining your approach to client interactions, negotiation, and deal-closing. A sales coach offers constructive feedback on sales processes, identifying improvement areas and introducing effective techniques to enhance lead conversion efficiency.

**Mindset Coach**: Focuses on cultivating a positive, growth-oriented mindset to overcome mental barriers and self-limiting beliefs. Employing a range of techniques, they work to build resilience, confidence, and motivation, preparing you mentally to tackle challenges and seize opportunities.

**Neuro-Linguistic Programming (NLP) Coach**: Uses NLP principles to foster positive changes in communication patterns, thought processes, and behaviors. These techniques improve relationships with clients and colleagues, boost persuasion and influence skills, and align subconscious patterns with conscious intentions for personal and professional growth.

**Leadership Coach**: Aims to develop your leadership skills, helping you to inspire and guide teams more effectively. Whether you're leading a small team or an entire organization, a leadership coach works with you to refine your vision, communication, and decision-making skills, ensuring you're equipped to lead with confidence and integrity.

**Performance Coach**: Concentrates on enhancing your overall performance by setting and achieving higher standards in your work. They help you identify performance gaps, develop actionable strategies for improvement, and track your progress towards achieving your peak performance levels.

**Career Coach**: Assists you in navigating career transitions, identifying opportunities for growth, and developing strategies for career advancement. They provide valuable insights into aligning your skills and passions with potential career paths, resume building, and interview preparation.

**Life Coach**: Offers guidance in achieving personal fulfillment and balance in addition to professional success. They address broader aspects of your life, helping you to articulate and achieve personal goals, improve relationships, and find greater satisfaction in daily life.

Each type of coach offers distinct benefits, enabling you to address a wide spectrum of personal and professional challenges. By engaging with the right coach or combination of coaches, you're not just investing in your immediate development but laying the groundwork for sustained excellence and success in your field. This tailored, comprehensive approach ensures you continue to build upon the momentum gained from your self-directed learning efforts, propelling you towards achieving your full potential.

## Keep it simple

As you apply what you learned, remember the following essential elements of crafting a sales strategy for law firms with this simple list.

**Brand Perception:** Craft a compelling brand that reflects your firm's values, expertise, and unique selling proposition to shape positive client perceptions.

**Targeted Marketing:** Identify ideal client personas and tailor marketing efforts, content, and messaging to resonate with their needs and preferences.

**Online Presence:** Optimize your website for lead generation and conversion, integrating tracking tools, live chat, and user-friendly forms for seamless interaction.

**Multi-channel Approach:** Strategically utilize various marketing channels such as Google Ads, social media, directories, and traditional media, aligning messaging to reach a wider audience.

**Reputation Management:** Monitor and manage your firm's online and offline reputation diligently, ensuring that your advertised claims align with client feedback and experiences.

**Exceptional Service:** Prioritize exceptional client service and support to enhance customer satisfaction, as positive experiences often lead to referrals and repeat business.

**Automation and Follow-up:** Implement automation tools like CRMs and email marketing for efficient lead nurturing, follow-ups, and maintaining client engagement.

**Continuous Improvement:** Regularly analyze marketing performance metrics and adapt strategies to remain agile, keeping up with industry trends and evolving client needs.

**Connect with Empathy:** Potential new customers feel valued, understood, and supported when you connect to their emotions. These feelings make them more likely to choose your firm over competitors.

Your firm's success hinges on the perception you craft before potential clients make contact. Your brand, encompassing reputation, aesthetics, and messaging, are the cornerstone of this perception. Nurturing a compelling brand narrative isn't just about visibility. It's about building trust and credibility.

Carefully selecting marketing channels aligned with your brand ethos amplifies your impact. Consistency in messaging across platforms resonates with your ideal clientele, drawing them closer to your firm. Monitoring and managing your firm's reputation are non-negotiables. Ensure every client interaction aligns with your advertised claims, bridging the gap between expectation and reality to foster enduring trust.

Exceptional service isn't just a differentiator. It's your best marketing strategy. Prioritize client experience and invest in robust customer support to reinforce your brand's reliability. As you forge ahead armed with the insights gleaned from these pages, weave these practices into the fabric of your firm's culture. Embrace change, adapt to evolving trends, and always put the client journey at the forefront.

May this book serve as the game-changing catalyst in your law firm's sales journey, inspiring you to ascend to new heights of success. May it ignite your enthusiasm for mastering the nuanced art of legal sales and motivate you to transform into a more empowered and persuasive version of yourself. Here's to you becoming a paragon of industry leadership, widely acclaimed for your innovative approach to client-centricity and mastery of sales.

Know that by mastering the insights within this book and achieving your individual success, you become a key player in the collective movement toward transforming the legal industry that inspired the creation of this book. Together we're not just aiming for personal triumphs. We're striving to shift the legal landscape from a realm often perceived as apathetic and cold to one that radiates warmth and trustworthiness. Your success and the excellence you demonstrate become beacons, inspiring change and encouraging a more empathetic, client-centered approach across the industry.

As you apply the *Connect Convert* strategies to connect with others and convert more leads into signed cases, you are ultimately enhancing people's lives. Imagine yourself redefining the legal industry so it becomes a place where every client feels genuinely understood, valued, and supported. By integrating these strategies, you're not just offering legal services; you're providing a beacon of hope and trust. Your application of these principles sets a new standard in legal practice, where clients don't just receive representation but gain a steadfast ally. Thank you for reading this book and following it up with your best effort to light the path to a future where the legal profession is celebrated for its compassion and integrity, truly impacting the lives of those who deserve nothing less.

# Margarita Eberline

Margarita Eberline is a transformative figure in law firm marketing and sales. As the founder of Marketing Boss, a distinguished fractional CMO company, she empowers law firm owners to plan and execute effective marketing strategies and achieve unparalleled success.

With an extensive career of more than 25 years, Margarita has mastered tailoring marketing strategy and implementation solutions. Her expertise has been honed through her invaluable contributions to renowned companies such as Telemundo, The Nielsen Company, Columbia Pictures, and KNBC in Los Angeles, as well as a media agency owner.

Margarita's passion is providing business owners comprehensive insights and unwavering support in marketing and business growth through her company, Marketing Boss. By leveraging her guidance, law firms can maximize their potential, scale their operations faster, and achieve remarkable results more easily.

Recognized as a highly sought-after international public speaker, Margarita captivates audiences with her profound insights and dynamic presence. In addition to her speaking engagements, Margarita extends her knowledge and expertise through workshops, conferences, digital courses, and tutorials. She is also an avid blogger, covering various topics that include marketing, sales, leadership, and inspiration. Her thought-provoking content resonates with readers, inspiring them to achieve their fullest potential with less stress and more fun.

When she is not busy being a boss at the office, Margarita enjoys an active lifestyle as a boss mom of five young boys. Balancing her roles as a successful entrepreneur and a devoted mother, she finds solace in contributing to non-profit organizations that align with her journey as a survivor of childhood domestic violence. Drawing inspiration from her own life experiences, Margarita strives to transform lives through the power of businesses and communities.

# Endorsements

### T. Jayden Doyé, Law Firm CPA

Margarita is a very talented CMO. She uses her knowledge from corporate America to help firm owners grow and scale easily. Her compassion, paired with her love of data, is what sets her apart from her competition. Her talent is being able to customize a plan for her client's marketing using historical data that falls in line with their long-term goals.

### Roger Ponce, Trial Attorney/CEO Ponce Law

I must say, her talents and qualities truly shine through in various aspects. I've observed that she possesses a remarkable, captivating, and inspiring energy. Her expertise in marketing is evident, but what truly sets her apart is her ability to bring out the best in individuals and effectively represent their aspirations. Her talent for understanding and conveying their goals is truly remarkable.

Moreover, her proficiency in organizing, implementing, and measuring results showcases her dedication and skill in managing projects successfully. In my opinion, her presence is an invaluable asset to any management team. Her capability to handle responsibilities and demonstrate effective management is vital in receiving blessings and achieving success.

### Russell Taylor, Attorney Daniels & Taylor P.C.

Margarita Eberline's law firm sales strategies are outstanding! Her succinct and easily digestible insights have empowered our team to communicate our value more confidently. Her strategies for building trust, enhancing client connections, and boosting case sign-ups are transformative. This book is an indispensable resource for legal professionals aiming to excel in a competitive market.

## Noemi Puntier, Founder Punter Law

The alignment of Margarita Eberline's principles with our commitment to delivering an exceptional customer service experience has yielded remarkable results. Not only have the insights from her book validated our current strategies, but they have also introduced innovative concepts that have significantly enhanced our sales and intake procedures. At Puntier Law, our dedication to prioritizing the customer is unwavering, and the invaluable teachings of Margarita Eberline have played a pivotal role in elevating our ability to provide unparalleled service.